The Worldwide Workplace

The Worldwide Workplace

Solving the Global Talent Equation

By
Mike Johnson

© Mike Johnson 2014

All rights reserved. No reproduction, copy or transmission of this publication may be made without written permission.

No portion of this publication may be reproduced, copied or transmitted save with written permission or in accordance with the provisions of the Copyright, Designs and Patents Act 1988, or under the terms of any licence permitting limited copying issued by the Copyright Licensing Agency, Saffron House, 6–10 Kirby Street, London EC1N 8TS.

Any person who does any unauthorized act in relation to this publication may be liable to criminal prosecution and civil claims for damages.

The author has asserted his right to be identified as the author of this work in accordance with the Copyright, Designs and Patents Act 1988.

First published 2014 by
PALGRAVE MACMILLAN

Palgrave Macmillan in the UK is an imprint of Macmillan Publishers Limited, registered in England, company number 785998, of Houndmills, Basingstoke, Hampshire RG21 6XS.

Palgrave Macmillan in the US is a division of St Martin's Press LLC, 175 Fifth Avenue, New York, NY 10010.

Palgrave Macmillan is the global academic imprint of the above companies and has companies and representatives throughout the world.

Palgrave® and Macmillan® are registered trademarks in the United States, the United Kingdom, Europe and other countries.

ISBN 978–1–137–36126–4

This book is printed on paper suitable for recycling and made from fully managed and sustained forest sources. Logging, pulping and manufacturing processes are expected to conform to the environmental regulations of the country of origin.

A catalogue record for this book is available from the British Library.

A catalog record for this book is available from the Library of Congress.

Typeset by MPS Limited, Chennai, India.

To my wife Julie and son Cameron for not asking "how's the writing going?" and my sincere excuses to Caesar for ignoring his pleas for walks!

Contents

Acknowledgments / viii

Introduction / 1

1 The Century of Uncertainty / 4

2 Seeking Out Work Opportunities / 30

3 People, Positions and Places / 58

4 What the Workplace Looks Like / 83

5 Making a Career Inside or Outside the Organization / 110

6 Educate, Educate, Educate / 150

7 The Organizational Challenges / 169

8 The Workplace of the Future, or More of the Same? / 196

Index / 205

Acknowledgments

There are many people who help to make a book work. In this case, a huge thanks to all those I interviewed and all those who have helped with input and ideas. Without them this book just wouldn't have happened. There are about 50 people who form the core material for this book. To make it fair, I've listed you all alphabetically – there are no favorites in the workplace of tomorrow; as in this book, we are all contributors and collaborators.

Dave Altman of the Center for Creative Leadership, for his views on tomorrow's organizational challenges + Khalid Aziz and his insights into job interviews + Adam Benthem, for an up-to-date view of the job marketplace + Andrew Chadwick, architect and office of the future pioneer + Andres Correa of AISEC + Richard Corliss, for his lobbying as a career expertise + Eric Cornuel, the Director General of EFMD, for insights into where the business school is going + Charlotte Crossley of Innovation Birmingham + Luc De Jaeger of Nexum Consulting + Cliff Dennett of Soshi Games, for a lot of useful ideas + Ben Emmens with insights into the Aid Sector as a career choice + Cristina Fancello of Generation Europe Foundation + Patrick Faniel of UBIS University + Hanneke Frese, super-coach extraordinaire! + Labeed Hamid, the Middle East workplace insights were invaluable + Sami Hamid, and your China experience + Tom Harnish, who knows a lot about tomorrow + Alain Haut, helpful views on the education system + Arnaud Houdmont, pleased that you now have that job you wanted! + Göran Hultin, for your wisdom + Susan Huskisson, I'd never go to

Acknowledgments

an interview without talking to you first + Malcolm Johnson of Atlas Consulting on expatriate developments + Elisabeth Kelan, author of *Rising Stars* and one herself + Peter Lorange, my favorite dean of all time + Anthony McAlister, sane thoughts about recruitment and careers + Jens Maier, a leader of the "just do it" generation + Sunita Malhotra, for insights on people development + Shay McConnon, fighting to make everywhere an *Even Better Place to Work* + Sandy McLean, keeping me straight on social media + Matthias Moelleney of PeopleXpert, great insight into job creation + Chiara Palieri, your enthusiasm is catching! + Rudi Plettinx for his views on leadership expectations + Jim Prouty, bringing an understanding of the microloan industry + "Dr Dave" Richards, for help on the concept of profiling + Helen Routledge, serious games expert + Catherine Russ, on the aid sector's future + Richard Savage, talking up the talent + Richard Smith of Totem Learning + Susan Stucky, helping me understand the way the workplace is going + Amrit Thind, for encapsulating the views of the NEXT Generation + Laurence VanHee, for spreading happiness + Atanaska Varbanova of Think Young + Peter Vogel, youth champion and serial entrepreneur, for showing how to do it + Jim Ware, for thoughts on the future workplace + Aaron White of the Center for Creative Leadership, for sharing his views of how to build a career. I'd also like to mention my thanks to Manpower Inc for allowing me to use some of their research.

I would also like to personally thank all the Partners of the FutureWork Forum, the think tank that I created with several colleagues back in 2003. I am delighted to say that every one of the 26 members of the FutureWork Forum has made a contribution to the book, bringing a depth of knowledge and experience that makes the content both relevant and unique. Chairing the FutureWork Forum has been one of the most rewarding parts of my professional career and has allowed me to work and learn from a wonderful group of people.

Introduction

The century that began on 1 January 2000 has already carved out a name to define itself – the Century of Uncertainty. Indeed, if you look at the collective headlines of the world's media, you could on a bad day be forgiven for thinking that the four horsemen of the Apocalypse (conquest, war, famine and death) had really taken over our planet. Conflict and natural disasters seem to dominate, closely followed by crashing financial markets and seemingly unending and unsolvable economic, social and environmental woes. Putting it simply – it's very easy to get depressed at the state of our world. Nothing, it would seem, is going quite the way we'd like it. We are constantly (and almost gleefully) informed that we are increasingly obese, face increasing costs in taxation and energy bills, have produced children who will struggle to find any kind of economic balance, while our planet gets warmer and the natural world shrivels up around us as a consequence of our massive population growth.

Today, we are told we inhabit a VUCA world – a time that is volatile, uncertain, complex and ambiguous. This means that we have to thrive and survive in a state of constant turbulence – a permanent white-water ride to some, as yet unknown, destination.

And yet we live amid unprecedented wealth. We create and use the most sophisticated equipment ever. We have healthcare that has advanced life expectancy by decades in less than half a century. And 50 years ago – when I was in school – it would have been impossible to imagine living in an age where every question known to man could be answered by a small device that fits into your pocket. A device that also allows you to text or talk with the other seven billion mobile devices that now surpass the number of people on this globe of ours. That sort of thing was for Buck Rogers and Dan Dare and the realm of boy's science-fiction comics.

Certainly it's easy to wallow in doom and gloom. There's no doubt that we have not been the most caring custodians of our home sphere, or learned how to live peaceably with each other, or provide basic food and shelter for everyone. But, in the midst of these travails and troubles, we do have a choice. Should we look at the glass as half-empty or half-full; are we going to be pessimistic or optimistic?

Without avoiding the harsh realities, this book sets out to take the half-full glass and fill it up. The reason? There's enough bad news, so there isn't much point in creating a book about it – that's not going to help anyone. What the next 70,000 or so words set out to do is make some sense of one part of our environment – the working world and the people who work in it. Like everything else it too is changing: new ways of working, new jobs, new places to work, new technologies to embrace that free us to do things in more productive and creative ways.

To do that, we are going to explore together the state of the working world and the likely outcomes over the coming years. Above all, we are going to look at it in a practical, people-driven way. We don't want the formulas and models in here; we want the reality of the real-life workplace.

> NOTE: This book is designed to help individuals in understanding job opportunities and also to let managers and business leaders understand the impact of the emerging world of work on their business. Therefore, Chapter 2, "Seeking Out Work Opportunities," offers insights for the individual reader, but also provides a context for how best to recruit, reward and retain employees.

Chapter 1: Provides a snapshot of the worldwide workplace today and the challenges that it brings to all of us by highlighting some of the key demographics that impact the working world.

Chapter 2: Examines the opportunities that the new world of work offers us – both as individuals and as organizations. It shows that while some doors are closing, others are opening – it's just a matter of finding the handle to open them up.

Chapter 3: Has two key roles to play. First, who is going to be in the workplace of the future and, second, what kind of jobs are there going to be and why?

Chapter 4: Investigates what the "physical" workplace will be like, what skills will be required and what kind of people we will need in order to grow and prosper in this new world of work environments.

Chapter 5: Illustrates how to develop a 21st-century career plan. What are you going to have to do to make it as you climb the world-of-work success ladder?

Chapter 6: Looks at different aspects of education – getting the formula right to meet the workplace needs of the future.

Chapter 7: Explains what organizations need to do to be successful in the new world of work. The challenges of recruiting, rewarding and retaining the talent they need.

Chapter 8: Offers some thoughts on the workplace of the future, some ideas of tomorrow's working world.

In all of this we are focused on being resolutely upbeat and seeking out the positives rather than the negatives. The idea is for you to close the book and feel that you have not only learned some useful things but have been energized and given a sense of purpose. Not only will you have a clear idea of the world of work, but an action plan to make it work for you and your organization – however big or small that may be.

Obviously, a single book cannot cover every last area of such a vast subject. So I have been selective in choosing examples that I feel provide the right sort of input that makes it clear where the working world is going, why it is happening and what the long-term outcomes are going to be. Also, I have concentrated in the main on the impact of the new world of work from a Western point of view.

We are off on a journey to see what the global world of work is really like. I hope you enjoy the ride.

Chapter 1
The Century of Uncertainty

There are a lot of people on this little planet of ours. In the time period it took me to write the first draft of this book (30 days), the number of people populating the Earth rose from 7,174,521,162 to 7,183,196,576.[1] That's 8,675,414 additional people! If you'd like another alarming statistic, despite famine, war and pestilence, we are incredibly good at producing people. From 1804 to 2011 we managed to increase the world's population from one billion to seven billion – and it's only going to take another 15 years to get to eight billion. The big issue is that a very large proportion of them would like a job. More than that, in even the most inhospitable spots, we are living a good deal longer. In Western Europe life expectancy rose from 47 in 1900, to 67 in 1950 and now it is 80. In mega-rich Monaco, citizens and tax exiles alike can expect to go on counting their coinage to a world-beating 89.5 years. There's just one problem: in most developed countries the population is in decline. We of the industrialized nations live longer but have fewer offspring – we're too busy working to have babies. In some places around this overcrowded globe of ours the decline is almost climatic as countries run out of people to do the jobs that keep society's wheels in motion.

---

[1] United Nations Development Programme (UNDP), www.worldometers.info/world-population.

The upshot of these developments is a massive and ongoing reduction in young people entering the job market (although you'll have a hard time convincing the youth of Greece, Spain, Ireland and Portugal of this) and a storm surge of elderly people. Already over 50 percent of the population of the world's developed countries are in the two so-called dependent groups (under 15 and over 64). Look at this table as an eye-opener of where we are:

Projected Change in Working-Age Population				
Region	1995	2010	2025	2050
Europe (millions)	486	496	452	370
World (billions)	3.5	4.5	5.3	6.0
Europe share %	14	11	9	6

Source: International Conference of Population and Development

As the old-age population rises, the working-age group shrinks. By 2030 the European workforce will be around 280 million, compared with around 300 million in 2011. This means that the European Union (EU) member states will need to import a vast army of new workers (estimates suggest 150 million over 20 years, giving the lie to the idea of rampant, uncontrolled immigration as being a very bad thing) just to maintain the present levels of service and support tax revenues that keep the whole machine going. Into that mix goes the fact that countries will be forced to raise retirement ages for their citizens from the current average of 65 to around 70 and more. This is already happening in many countries, despite the squeals of protest from the citizenry.

The demographic time bomb that is Europe, is mirrored in the US, where in 2013 labor-force growth was zero and expected to reverse (suggesting a shortage of working-age people of around 17 million by 2020). Some industries in the US are already in crisis. The medical profession has shortfalls of thousands of nurses and doctors.[2]

---

[2] The problem is that if a country imports a large number of nurses and doctors from overseas there is a knock-on effect in the country these people come from. This was seen in the UK with an aggressive recruitment campaign of nurses from the Philippines, which spiked a nursing crisis back home as Filipino nurses leapt at the opportunity to earn higher wages.

Engineering firms across the US have reported a need to invest in new, robotic machinery (not new employees) because they can't get the skilled workers they need.

Just to get you in the mood for what comes next, here are a few more demographic facts and figures to illustrate that the world of work and the global jobs market is about to become very interesting indeed. Or perhaps that word "uncertain" would be more appropriate:

- Japan's population is falling off the proverbial cliff. Current estimates show today's population of 127 million declining to 107 million by 2040 and shrinking dramatically further to just 87 million by 2060 Worse still, by then, just 50 percent of the population will be in the working-age category. This puts a country that has a fairly xenophobic attitude to foreigners seriously on the back foot. Population experts calculate that Japan would have to import over half a million immigrants every year just to maintain the current size of its working population. That shows no sign whatsoever of happening.
- Despite some recent economic woes, China is short of 10 to 12 million workers. And in a mind-boggling statistic, the UN has predicted that by 2040 the Chinese will have 400 million citizens over 65, a group larger than the combined populations of France, Germany, Italy, Japan and the UK.
- Across the rest of Asia, national governments are waking up to a maturing population and flatlining or collapsing birth rates. Soon they will face similar choices to the West.
- Australians – always prepared to be different – are averse to working past retirement. Just 49 percent of workers between 55 and 64 work, compared with 59 percent in the US and 65 percent in Scandinavia.
- The German Institute for Economic Research suggests that there may be as many as 50,000 of what it terms "missing" engineers. This is a direct result of a concern years ago that engineers were not needed and Germans chose to train for other occupations. This is

called getting the job pipeline very wrong indeed. Elsewhere, the small and medium-sized enterprise (SME) sector (the backbone of Germany's economy) reports that four out of every five firms experience difficulties in getting the skilled people they require.

- Also, German SMEs are discovering that the current generation of the family are not that interested in going into the family firm (a situation mirrored across the EU and the US) and are creating a new uncertainty about how they will organize themselves in the future.
- The great Russian bear is bucking for cuddly toy status – shrinking before our eyes. From a peak of 147 million some years ago, there are now 143 million citizens, but this number is predicted to fall by a full 20 percent, to 111 million by 2050. Concerns that the once mighty Russian state will turn into a pipsqueak nation have prompted President Putin to call for cash incentives for couples to have more than one child.
- Germany faces the same population shrinkage as Russia. By 2050 the population is expected to reduce from today's 82 million to around 70 million. Also, the population distribution will look very different in 2050 – mainly, much older. Whereas there are around 50 million people of working age (20–64) living in Germany today, this figure will drop to between 36 and 39 million by 2050. The average German by then will be 50 years old.
- While Japan, Russia and Germany face a shrinking citizenry, the United Kingdom faces the opposite – a population explosion. Current estimates suggest that the population is on course to reach 73 million by 2035. Just over two-thirds of the projected increase from 2010 to 2035 is either directly or indirectly due to migration. This will be due to people entering the UK, and also their future offspring. The UK is regarded as the most popular place in Europe to try and build a life and this shows no sign of diminishing anytime soon.

What all this clearly illustrates is that individual nations and whole regions are in a constant state of flux. More than that, to survive in anything like their present form, many countries are going to have to get a whole lot better at two things – immigration and outsourcing. Immigration because their ageing populations will force them to import talent to keep the nation-state alive, and outsourcing to other countries that can do many of the jobs that need to be done to keep the country operational.

The migrant mix

Migration has been a part of human history forever. Whole populations, persecuted peoples and those seeking a better stake in life have constantly changed the make-up of the world. Today, economic migrants – those who make a choice to move somewhere, as opposed to those who move because they have no other choice – make up a broad group. They bring all sorts of needed skills to all sorts of places.

When it comes to jobs, we tend to think at two ends of the spectrum: the so-called brain drain where scientists and highly qualified professionals move around the globe offering their services to the highest bidder; and, at the lower end, of the likes of Indian and Pakistani construction workers in the Middle East, working on possibly unsafe and unsupervised construction sites.

But, despite all the media frenzy built around foreigners coming into our countries and taking our jobs, they are – in reality – a fairly small group of migrants, compared with those who choose to stay at home.

Currently, there are around 200 million people (about 3 percent of the world's total population) living outside their country of birth (accurate figures are difficult to calculate). This is about double the amount of 1985. Demographers suggest that most immigrants move to developed countries and that this will result in an average gain of around two million people every year until 2050.

But migration is not confined to the one-way street of poor country to rich country. In the UK, 1.5 million graduates left to seek out opportunities in the US, Canada, Australia and the European Union.

This compares with the 1.3 million graduates who came to the UK in the same period in search of better jobs. While the UK may be growing in population and is a real talent magnet for job seekers, it also exports one in six of its graduates. On the other hand, in France (which has the lowest migration rate of any OECD country), only 1 in 30 leave the home turf. This may have something to do with language – English being the lingua franca of commerce. It pays to remember that there is always a good reason for a statistic!

Massive shortages

As we saw earlier with the Filipino nurses streaming to UK hospitals and creating a massive shortage in their own country, economic migration in search of that better job is plunging many emerging economies into deep trouble. According to the International Conference on Population and Development (ICPD), "poor countries across Africa, Central America and the Caribbean are losing sometimes staggering numbers of their college-educated workers to wealthy industrialized democracies." Researchers found that between a quarter and almost a half of the college-educated nationals of Ghana, Mozambique, Kenya, Uganda, Nicaragua and El Salvador live in the 34 OECD member states.[3] The ICPD report goes on to say that, "for Haiti and Jamaica the number rises to more than 80 percent. In contrast, less than five percent of the skilled nationals of the great behemoths of the developing world – India, China, Indonesia and Brazil – live in a member country."

Such is the impact of foreign workers doing jobs in developed countries that the health sector now employs 21 percent of all foreign workers in Norway, 19 percent in Sweden, 14 percent in the UK, 12 percent in the Netherlands and 11 percent in the US.

---

[3] ICPD report: "Employment Trends in the 21st Century", 2011. The OECD is the rich nations' country club, headquartered in Paris's toney 16th arrondissement. Twenty countries originally signed the Convention on the Organization for Economic Co-operation and Development on 14 December 1960. Since then a further 14 countries have become members of the organization.

However, there is good news too. A World Bank report shows that immigrants repatriating money earned from these overseas jobs have substantially reduced poverty in countries such as Mexico, Guatemala and the Philippines. Indeed, Romania now receives more than five billion euros a year from workers employed in the EU.

Again according to the ICPD, these are just the most visible parts of a reverse brain drain. They say that this diaspora brings four other key benefits to these emerging countries:

- It spurs the transfer of technology and business practices back to the home country.
- The immigrants ignite the growth of business back home.
- Migration of talent overseas creates job opportunities in the domestic market, raises domestic salary scales and motivates others to upgrade their knowledge and skills.
- In the next stage, foreign companies implant their operations in the migrants' home country to access local talent without moving them overseas.

But there is one other thing to keep in mind; in most developed countries the citizens don't move very much at all. Indeed, according to studies in the EU countries, most European nationals are born, grow up, build a life and die within 100 kilometers of their birthplace.

The great visa question

Such are the mixed messages surrounding the immigration issue that many countries – with very real talent shortages – are in danger of strangling economic opportunity, due to political and societal pressures about the number of "foreigners coming into our country and taking our jobs."

There is little doubt that governments need to take a much more pragmatic view of bolstering the talent pipeline if they dare (knowing how many votes it may well cost them if they do). In the US, the chief executives of Facebook, Google, Yahoo! and others complain that they cannot find the talent they need within their domestic borders. But, with the US visa program to recruit foreign technical specialists capped at 65,000 people a year, it is hard to see how they can overcome the problem. The visa cap is exceeded within days of each year's visa quota opening up. There are similar stories from other developed nations, pointing to a very real need to create new rules on these issues if countries are not to strangle the ability of companies to develop for the good of the national economy. Amazingly, one of our featured growth of jobs areas (see later) doesn't have this problem.

Countries to work in

It's not only those smart, well-educated graduates from Africa, South America and the Caribbean who are flocking to the OECD's member countries either. A new professional class, at home almost anywhere in the world, has also been on the lookout for the best places to work, especially those where there is an ideal work–life balance (of which more in Chapter 3). While regular surveys by magazines and polling firms that rate countries and cities regularly put New Zealand, Australia, Canada, Switzerland and the Scandinavian quartet at the top of their "Where to Live" wish lists, the global professional eyes up the possibilities in a way that balances a good income and good lifestyle with the challenges that work will bring.

London-based recruiter Hydrogen polled 2353 internationally operating professionals,[4] asking them where they would prefer to live and work. Remember these are members of the international business class, who want challenge, income and a lifestyle that meets their requirements. The choices explain a lot:

1. United States   13%
2. Australia   9%
3. United Kingdom   9%

---

[4] "Global Professionals on the Move – 2012," Hydrogen.

4. Singapore   6%
5. Canada   5%
6. Switzerland 4%
7. Hong Kong   4%
8. France   4%

Just 2 percent suggested China. These are interesting results when you consider where people want to go and where the right kind of infrastructure coupled to career challenge exists. Being honest, China may be the great new frontier, but it is just that – a frontier too far for those really sophisticated global managers who can choose where they live and how they manage their jobs.

And international experience is seen increasingly by many industries as a key to success – more so than simply having good technical knowledge of your profession. According to the Hydrogen report, international experience was cited as a very important attribute by 76 percent of those in the energy industry, 73 percent in pharmaceuticals, 69 percent in law and 62 percent in finance.

Vocational skills in demand

Demand for skills is everywhere. And when it comes to the kind of jobs, the variety is astounding. Global people provider Manpower report that the global top ten jobs that employers are having difficulty filling are, in order of scarcity:[5]

1. Skilled Trade Workers (plumbers, carpenters, electricians etc.)
2. Engineers
3. Sales Representatives
4. Technicians
5. Accounting and Finance Staff
6. Management Executives
7. IT Staff

---

[5] "2013 The Great Talent Shortage Awakening," Manpower Inc.

8. Drivers
9. Secretaries, PAs, Administration Assistants and Office Support Staff
10. Laborers

Obviously, these demands rise and fall depending on the country, but it still shows that there are a huge number of trades and professions where shortages are endemic.

Göran Hultin, a global labor consultant and a former deputy director general of the International Labour Organization (ILO), adds emphasis to Manpower's findings on talent shortages: "Globally, one employer in three cannot find the skills they need – and it is not only about university graduates. In almost all labor markets the most difficult to find professionals are the vocationally skilled ones."

This is an important point to take on board. We have created a society where academic paths are more valued by society than vocational ones. The few exceptions are countries such as Austria, Germany and Switzerland with their long-term belief in the apprenticeship system. If you compare unemployment and growth statistics in this triumvirate with those of other nations the results are most interesting and point to why others are now embarking on their own – but often less onerous – versions of the apprenticeship system.

Seeking out new talent

With shortages of talent abounding, job industry experts are counseling that organizations large and small are going to have to look for the people they need in entirely new places. Manpower Inc contends that "87 percent of companies experiencing a talent shortage are not actively looking for new sources of talent." Manpower add, "Women and young people, for example, make up a considerable proportion of the world's population and untapped sources of talent, but only a tiny fraction of shortage-affected employers are actively seeking to recruit them. This makes little sense. Effectively tapping into these 'new' sources of talent will place an organization leagues ahead of its competitors."

They're right. But sadly, most organizations suffer from what I have for decades labeled as the "different kind of Bob" syndrome. Many companies agree that they should diversify the employee mix, but culturally they are just unable to do it. French firms have French citizens in top positions, so do Germans, Swedes, Japanese and Brazilians. Firms hire headhunters with instructions to "scour the ends of the earth" for great talent. But when it comes to the crunch of hiring they fall back into the "safe mode" of bringing on board a clone of themselves. Yes, a "different kind of Bob, Miguel, Helmut, or Jaques."[6]

Equally, when it comes to searching out new talent, organizations seem very reluctant to tread new paths, break new ground and explore different avenues of opportunity. Certainly we have US, UK and German bankers using Polish and Hungarian workers in Poland and Hungary for their back-office operations. But this isn't much of a change. The people they use are just wannabe versions of themselves, who think the same things, dress the same way and have essentially the same training. But no one is looking outside these safe new corridors to seek out what would be regarded as the unusual and exotic. There is a lot of talent out there that would just love the opportunity. The trouble is it doesn't know how to reach out and get that job and we don't know how to get to these people. As one of the people who defined and described the 19th century explained:

> There are all kinds of employers wanting all sorts of people and all sorts of people wanting all kinds of employers – and they never seem to come together.

Dickens wrote these words sometime around 1840. The fact that we still struggle, 170-plus years later, to match people who need jobs

---

[6] Back in the 1990s I carried out a study that tracked the make-up of a range of global corporations, using their annual reports as the base. Over a period of five years, less than 8 percent appointed anyone outside of their own comfort zone to a senior management position. The conclusion? White American, French and German managers etc. hired clones of themselves – it makes them feel safe. So, by the way, do the Russians, Japanese, Chinese, Brazilians … and the rest.

with people who have them to offer shows that our inability to solve pressing problems has a long, long history. Solving the global talent equation is blocked by our own inbuilt habits and historical prejudices.

And what of the robot?

We have already mentioned how engineering firms in the US are being forced to rely on robotics to counter the shortage of machine operators. Well it's not only in engineering that this is occurring. What's really worrying is whether technical advances are having a real effect on the overall jobs market. Two Massachusetts Institue of Technology (MIT) / Sloan School of Management professors, Erik Brynjolfsson and Andrew McAfee, contend that major advances in computer technology (from industrial robotics to automated translation services) are one of the consequences of the sluggish employment growth of the last decade.[7] And they affect a lot more than engineering jobs – clerical, retail, legal and financial services, education and medicine are all in the frame.

"New technologies are encroaching into human skills in a way that is completely unprecedented," say Brynjolfsson and McAfee, and many middle-class jobs are on the line. "The middle seems to be going away," they add, "the top and bottom are clearly getting further apart."

That we are seeing the rise of a new society where the middle is missing is also noted by MIT economist David Autor: "Computers have increasingly taken over tasks like bookkeeping, clerical work and the repetitive production-line tasks." These are the "jobs" that once provided respectable lower-middle-class employment. "At the same time," explains Autor, "higher-paying jobs requiring creativity and problem-solving skills – often aided by computers – have proliferated. But so have low skill jobs that can't be automated – waiters, cooks, janitors and other service workers. The result has been a polarization of the workforce

---

[7] Erik Brynjolfsson and Andrew McAfee, *Race against the Machine: How the Digital Revolution is Accelerating Innovation, Driving Productivity, and Irreversibly Transforming Employment and the Economy*, Digital Frontier Press, Lexington, MA, 2012, www.raceagainstthemachine.com.

and a hollowing out of the middle class." Certainly if you think about it, that's exactly what we have been witnessing during this last decade – it's just that no one has really drawn our attention to it before now.

New jobs: the mafia and aid workers

In my promise to leave no stone unturned and no corner unswept in seeking out the future of the workplace, I would be remiss indeed if I did not mention two areas where employment growth is booming, one of which (at the very least) offers for the future the prospect of middle-class respectability, stability and career opportunities.

The fact that these very different "industries" have a focus on the underdogs of our societies makes them a very strange pair indeed. They are also "industries" where a "frisson of fear" may be part of the package. In other words the work can have its hazardous moments, depending on which part you choose to play in it.

The first of our new job creators is the global operations of organized crime – an employment sector that, unseen by most of us, is in the midst of massive growth. Traditional areas of "work" – drugs, gambling, prostitution and money laundering – have, of late, been eclipsed by electronic and financial crime. Today, organized crime operations fall into the "iceberg employer" category: only about one-eighth (the nasty bits) is visible. The hoodlums, gunslingers and cyber-terrorists are backed up by the many thousands of people who make their living from organized crime without – often – knowing who they are really working for. Hundreds of job categories, from accountants to lawyers, from chefs and waiters to pilots and drivers, doctors and nurses, derive their uneventful middle-class existence from the well-oiled machinery of organized crime. Lately, computer crime has been high on the agenda, employing thousands of programmers, many of whom got their training in the Russian and Chinese military.

The leading group in organized crime at present (the Apple or Samsung of the underground industry) is the Russian mafia. Officially known as Russian Transnational Organized Crime (TNOC), it is suggested that it numbers around 300,000 employees – that makes it one of the world's largest corporations, even if it doesn't publish its annual turnover in *Fortune* magazine.

In typical "iceberg employer" mode, the Russian TNOC has combined street-level visible crime (such as human trafficking and drug smuggling) with less visible white collar crimes such as the counterfeiting of goods (cigarettes are highly popular) and tax evasion on an industrial scale. The Russian mafia have turned organized crime into a global business model and make full use of the dual and multiple nationality status of its members – a direct result of the breakup of the Soviet Union. In addition there are over a million former Soviet citizens residing in Israel with citizenship there, free to travel to the EU and the US without visas (Israelis have visa-free access to Russia too). The mafia also make extensive use of ethnic Russians with EU passports. This amazing access to talent, where and when you want it, would seem to be a far cry from Apple, Yahoo! and Facebook going through channels and petitioning the US government for a few more visas for much needed technical talent!

THE WORLD AS 100 PEOPLE

Imagine planet Earth, not as a swollen mass of seven billion-plus bodies, but just 100 souls. To give you an idea of how our world stacks up, here is who they are:

- Gender: 50 are male and 50 are female
- Age: 26 would be under 14; 66 would be 15 to 64; eight would be 65 or older
- Geography: 60 from Asia; 15 from Africa; 11 from Europe; nine from Latin America and the Caribbean; five from North America
- Religion: 33 Christian; 22 Muslim; 14 Hindu; seven Buddhist; 12 believe in other religions; 12 have no particular faith
- Language: 12 Chinese; five Spanish; five English; three Arabic; three Hindi; three Bengali; three Portuguese; two Russian; two Japanese; 62 speak other languages

- Literacy: 83 can read and write
- Education: 74 would have primary school education; 64 would have secondary education; eight have college degrees
- Urban / rural: 51 are urban dwellers
- Safe water: 87 would have access to safe drinking water
- Food: 15 would be undernourished
- Poverty: 48 would live on less than US$2 per day and one out of two children would live in poverty
- Electricity: 78 would have electricity
- Technology: 75 are cell phone users; 30 are active internet users; 22 would own or share a computer
- Sanitation: 65 would have improved sanitation; 16 would have no toilets

The third sector

The other big growth area is the international aid and development sector. As of 2013 it was estimated that there were approximately 75 million people around the globe in need of humanitarian assistance. Though figures are hard to come by, it is thought there are around a quarter of a million aid workers, comprising foreign aid workers and people from the countries directly affected. The largest organizations are several agencies of the UN and the Red Cross, but they are closely followed in numbers of employees by Save the Children, Oxfam, Caritas and World Vision.

Over the last decade these organizations have been working hard at creating a much more professional management structure – modeling themselves more and more on the private sector. Moreover, salaries and fringe benefits (such as pension plans, medical cover and working conditions) have been evolving increasingly in line with the lower end of for-profit business. In addition, competition for aid-sector cash has been ramped up as big corporations in areas such as logistics (think FedEx and DHL) and the big consulting firms (think Deloitte, PwC and KPMG) have realized that they can make money from humanitarian aid. As one senior aid expert put it, "Let's face it, if Procter & Gamble or Unilever can deliver UN food aid for less than a charity, who do you think will get the contract?"

But now the aid sector is poised for another boost in the numbers making up its ranks. In 2012 one of the leading aid organizations – Save the Children – carried out a study that showed that the number of people around the world who would be directly affected by climate change-driven disaster (earthquakes, floods, famines, tornados and so forth) was set to increase dramatically. Their thinking is that the number will change as follows:

Population Affected by Climate Disasters		
2004	2010	2015
110m	263m	375m

Source: Save the Children: Humanitarian & Leadership Academy 2012

Incredibly, the number of people affected just by climate change events more than trebles in a period of ten years. What's got the aid business all excited (or worried depending on your viewpoint) is that they are going to need an awful lot of people to manage and care for all these people when the inevitable happens, somewhere in the world. Furthermore, these huge affected populations do not include those displaced by wars and other man-made disasters.

What this means is that there will be two sorts of needs. First, for people to actually do stuff – everything from distributing supplies to finding new sources of water to securing the funding that makes it all happen. Second, for people to train those people to do the right sort of stuff. To make this happen, organizations such as Save the Children are putting huge resources into training and development, upskilling their existing people and looking around for new talent to help meet these emerging needs.

As pointed out earlier, the aid sector has been moving quietly toward a sort of parity in terms of compensation and benefits with at least some of the private organizations. This means that it is now perfectly possible for a smart young graduate, or an experienced manager who wants to do something different, to join an aid agency and build a viable, rewarding career. So more job opportunities are going to open up and there will be more challenges and pressures on the private sector in the search for talent. Jobs in the humanitarian aid sector aren't confined to sticking on bandages. Smart marketers, fund-raisers, logistics and finance experts as well as IT developers are all required – the same talents that the private firms need too. So another career opportunity opens up that will most certainly continue to grow as we seek to mitigate the effects of natural disasters on our global population.

Don't make your choice now – or whether you choose to join the ranks of the criminal underworld or an international aid agency – but these developments illustrate that whatever else, the opportunities for employment are very varied and forever evolving. Those pessimists who claim there are no opportunities are wrong – you just need to know where to look.

Educators have let down the NEXT generation

Talk to any employer practically anywhere in the world and you'll pick up a very strong sense of frustration when they talk about their hiring needs. Not only can they not track down the skilled professionals they need, but also they cannot find the right entry-level staff either. In the hundreds of discussions and interviews I've conducted in the process of preparing this book, it has become clear that the majority of young people leave school, college or university ill-prepared for a job in the real world. This is unfortunate. While we'll go into some of the reasons in more depth and look at how to change that in Chapter 5, let's now take a quick look at some of the issues.

According to a report by management consultants McKinsey,[8] over 70 percent of educational institutions claim that they turn out what

---

[8] "Education to Employment: Designing a System that Works," McKinsey & Company, 2012.

they term "employment-ready" graduates. This starry-eyed bunch of educators couldn't have got it more wrong, because just 42 percent of employers and 45 percent of young people agreed with them.

And I find – based on my own interviews – that employers and young job seekers think this number is already far too high. In a study I developed for the FutureWork Forum and the Generation Europe Foundation in 2010,[9] just one in every six of the so-called NEXT generation believed they were (or were currently being) given the required skills at school or college to get a job. This was a research survey based on a total of 7,062 responses from all over Europe.

Employers I talked with agreed. Most said that they take in young people and have to completely train them from the ground up. More than that, employers complain that these young people are often also lacking in so-called life skills (simple things such as how to open a bank account and balance a household budget).

In October 2013, while this book was being completed, automotive firm Jaguar Land Rover announced some good news for the hard-pressed British economy. They were adding 1700 new jobs at one of their factories. The only downer was an interview with the Jaguar Land Rover CEO, Ralph Speth, who voiced concerns that the problem would be finding the people to do the jobs. He indicated that the firm would most probably have to train everyone they took on.

No career guidance

There's worse to come. While being work-ready is obviously a problem for most graduates from education, the fact that they got little, if any, career guidance while they were at school is a further indictment of the system. Where there was some career guidance, survey participants reported that it was either irrelevant or totally out of date. Most respondents said that they wouldn't have used it even if it was on

---

[9] "Employing the NEXT Generation: The Right Skills in the Right Place at the Right Time," 2010.

offer, as career counselors had no idea of the current job market. How educators can ever crawl back from this state of affairs, frankly, beats me. Their refusal to change their own status quo has had a huge and extremely detrimental effect on a generation of ill-informed job seekers.

Having said that, many young people have only themselves to blame for facing a jobless future. Too many didn't read the signs of economic meltdown and persisted in a "head in the sand" ostrich display. When they should have been taking practical courses that would land them a job (e.g. law graduates always get hired to do something even if it has nothing to do with the law, because they have demonstrated they can excel at certain "must have" abilities), they were doing a degree in ancient history or veterinary science (do you know how many unemployed vets there are? I've lost count, although in some countries they are seen to be in increasing demand).

I recently met an angry young woman who was desperate for a career as a librarian. "That's what I want to be," she exclaimed. But in a real world of public funding cuts, with libraries closing rather than opening, is this really a sane career option? This attitude is sadly repeated in thousands of other "long past their sell-by date" jobs. The lesson here is simple – get real!

Also at fault was the social trend (already referred to) of everyone aspiring to a university degree, when a vocational qualification would not only have been more appropriate but possibly have led to a stable and well-paid job.

Many people I've talked to put part of the failure of this generation down to their parents:

- Unrealistic aspirations that their children should go to university.
- Failure to encourage them to find weekend and summer jobs to gain experience of real-life working.
- The fear of letting young people out on the streets, so a refusal to let them do newspaper rounds or other deliveries that provide a basic sense of responsibility.

While these could be contributory factors, the truth is that we have a generation that had more choice than any other, was linked up more than any other, but has failed to put it collectively together. While there are many young people with stellar careers ahead of them (and a lot of would-be entrepreneurs seeking to do it their own way), there are far too many who just don't have the skills (especially amidst recession) to help themselves out of trouble.

The "most powerful" generation

Not everyone agrees with the "it's just hopeless" scenario. Chiara Palieri, a bubbly young Neapolitan who has become a one-woman booster for today's youth, has a totally different take on where she and her colleagues are placed in the big scheme of things. Asked if she felt she was part of a "lost generation," Palieri replied, "I strongly believe I am part of the most powerful generation that ever existed. A generation which knows how to reinvent itself and manage to survive amidst highly challenging times." She continued, "Just take a look at all the amazing start-ups and social enterprises that have flourished even during this time of crisis."

As a vocal advocate for young people, who has spent many years attending conferences and seminars on youth issues, Palieri also has her view about who is to blame for the mess her parents' generation have got the youth of today into. "The blame," says Palieri, "has to be equally shared between business (which doesn't have youth-friendly schemes for employment), government (which fails to address or implement policies to ensure young people meaningful work experience) and educators." Of educators, Palieri says, "schools and universities do not equip students to become useful employees. Education should do a much better job of adapting to the reality of today's marketplace. They need to educate students to work within an ever-changing environment and train them about essential tools like social media and entrepreneurship."

In the street speak of the US, the NEXT generation are referred to as "Generation Screwed!" In a more dainty European way we call it the "lost generation." Either way, and despite the talent shortages, they are not finding it easy to get a job, mainly because they are not qualified to take up those on offer. As this book was being written, there were eye-popping levels of youth unemployment (over 50 percent in Greece and Spain). While politicians shake their heads and make grand speeches, this huge mass of unemployed are feeling deserted by authority. Perhaps the only bright thing on their horizon is that they are part of countries where the extended family is still a feature of the culture. In Spain and Greece, three and four generations live together. In both those countries the black economy (the one that doesn't show up in the monthly statistics) is alive and well. How much it alleviates the problems is difficult to say, but somewhere out there it is keeping people in the one thing they need, whether it is official or unofficial – a job.

In Ireland, where the 19th and 20th centuries had seen mass emigration, the Irish diaspora have been returning home in the past decade to feed the employment needs of the aggressively named Celtic Tiger. Now as the tiger sits whimpering in a corner, they are leaving again.

The sad fact is that in countries such as Spain and Ireland, many young people left school as soon as they could and went into the then booming construction industry. When the crisis hit, the industry collapsed practically overnight. This left thousands of young people not only jobless, but without any formal training or educational qualifications to enable them to pursue other areas of employment.

The level of desperation among young people in these countries to nail down a job – however ill-paid it might be – was all too neatly captured by the response to an advertisement in Spain for 11 low-level jobs as guards at Madrid's storied Prado art gallery. Although salaries were just €13,000 a year, a mind-boggling total of 18,524 people applied for the jobs.

The chances of landing a job in the European Union are put into stark reality by a Gallup / Debating Europe Poll that posed the question,

"Will young people have more or fewer opportunities than their parents' generation to have a secure job?"[10]

The pessimism is palpable:

Fewer Opportunities (than your Parents) to Find a Secure Job	
Poland	62%
Germany	62%
UK	63%
France	71%
Spain	78%
Italy	92%

Fewer Opportunities (than your Parents) to have a Secure Pension	
Poland	59%
UK	63%
Germany	69%
France	73%
Spain	81%
Italy	93%

No one bothered to ask the Greeks how they felt about all this.

Welcome the wirearchy

In much of this chapter we've taken technology as a given. It's there, we use it. It helps us do stuff. But we cannot ignore the fact that today's and tomorrow's technologies are forging new business and management styles. Those who peddle organizational models and leadership classes for a living need to be aware that there is what they would no doubt term a paradigm shift that has created a need for new kinds of thinking and decision-making. It would seem there is a new

---

[10] "Outlook for the Future of Europe's Younger Generation," 2013.

kid on the decision-making block – "wirearchy" has replaced hierarchy. The basics behind this are that today the social networks, which allow you to engage with the ideas and insights of many, trump the brilliance of any one person. Indeed, if you want to make sense of the complex world we live in you have to ask thousands for their input. The next skill is to be able to distil that into an actionable strategy.

Essentially, it goes back to the clever thought that began with the mobile revolution a decade ago, which went, "Why would I ask my boss when I can ask the person who knows the answer?" This idea was predicated on the fact that in the past when you had a problem at work, you asked your superior. With mobile communication you ask who you think will give you the best information – even if it is your drinking buddy who works for a rival organization.

Now, with the masses of information out there and so many people who can be easily asked for answers, the real winners – and the real 21st-century leaders – will be those who can take all this complexity, embrace it, make sense of it and distil it down to its simplest form. There's also something about sharing collaboration and co-creation of value, which we'll get to later. In a complex VUCA (volatile, uncertain, complex, ambiguous) world these are the attributes we need to see in those who guide our fortunes and generate our jobs.

Projects and the digital world dominate

In the jobs we do in the future one form will dominate. Harking back to the concept of the wirearchy, we are already there. Digital will drive everything we do in terms of our jobs and the whole of our work–life environment.

Susan Stucky is an expert on behavior at work. One of the founders of the Institute for Research on Learning in California, she now works for IBM at their research center in Almaden in San Jose, California, where she looks at the best, most productive ways to work. "I think that working digitally will be more pronounced than working remotely," she says. "Similarly, I think that it is the emphasis on projects – planning them, managing and executing them – that will dominate." She goes on, "That is to say business processes, which are getting more and more automated (as we already explained) will continue to recede from awareness."[11]

Stucky continues her thoughts about work and the workplace: "One thing that won't change is that work – despite all the new bells and whistles – is fundamentally social – whether you are doing something alone or not. For instance this book you are writing has to meet certain social norms and expectations. You have to interact collaboratively with those you interview as well as your editor and publisher in socially accepted ways, or it isn't going to work – even if you then write the manuscript all alone. But much, if not all of this interaction is digitally mediated. We do this across time and space, whether it is with someone in the next room or on the other side of the world."

Stucky adds to this by suggesting: "In the myriad work arrangements I have been part of, the question behind the scenes has always been around how work actually gets done. Not how it is supposed to get done, or how people who are going to do it say they get it done, but how it actually unfolds in reality. Call that work practice or ways and styles of working. It's where the rubber meets the road, so to speak. If you think about it, we are so often interested in the latest technology, the latest gadget or the coolest new workplaces that we forget they are all simply in the service of getting the work done – productively, efficiently, effectively and perhaps with a little sprinkling of creativity or innovation thrown in for good measure." Yes, this is the key; technology assists – but it is people who make things happen.

The digital workspace

By now Susan Stucky is into her stride and produces both examples and ideas about why we (still) go to work and why jobs for us humans

---

[11] This interview is based on a talk by Susan Stucky for the Workplace Strategy Summit in San Francisco in 2012. The IFMA Foundation, Houston, Texas, will publish the original presentation in book form, titled, *Workplace Strategy Summit 2012, Research in Action*.

are still one of the only games in town. So here's her take on work in the digital world we all now inhabit. "When the context of work changes, what changes in work practice take place – intended or not?" Here Stucky cites an example based on her own experiences of how this notion of inherently social, but digitally mediated, work plays out: "For several years, I led a team building work and learning environments in a virtual world (in this instance Second Life). I went to work most days in this digital space with my colleagues. The team included people on different continents, in different divisions, even different companies. And it also included people down the corridor from where I had plunged into the digital space we all occupied."

Stucky continues, "The sense – the sensation – was not of remoteness so much as that I was just going to work digitally, because I was working with other people on a project. We had a shared work context. The only difference was not that all the work was in the digital realm, but that virtual world supported rich social interaction. Now, wherever we look today, we have on our hands a huge wave of social businesses. In its simplest form it means trying to take direct advantage of social media by using it to get work done. What that really translates into is that people are expected (or just will) to shift more of their work from email to more collaborative, shared digital work environments. This is a dramatic change in work practice – both in terms of the kind of social interaction around work and its digital experience."

Stucky ends with a prediction, "This shift will most probably be as transformative of how work gets done as email was when it began, or," she says laughingly, "the advent of instant messaging within the enterprise – if anyone can still remember that!"

The dominant factor

But, in the final analysis, Stucky is adamant about one thing. Sure there will be this mega-shift to digital working, but it is the social aspects of work that will still be the dominant factor. As she points out, "People (lots of them anyway) like being around others when they are working – we are, after all, social animals. However much the digital working world frees us up to work wherever and whenever we like, we tend to herd together (think coffee shops, bars and the like). The sociality of people and the sociality of work (even if we are not doing the same work as the guy sitting next to us) will always prevail and will trump any attempt to move people out of their offices where they feel safe in a shared work environment."

There's a huge amount in Stucky's story that business leaders need to take into account as they plan the next steps in their organizational strategies. Moreover, there's a huge amount we as individuals need to take from this in terms of the optimum ways to work in the future. Yes, in the final analysis, it's all about getting work done. We could say that's what the job is all about. So we may work smarter, but not a lot has changed very fundamentally underneath. The digital revolution and global reach may change the surface activity somewhat, but they are just tools. We still have jobs to do, outcomes to achieve and those get done by people. Chapter 2 will explain more about what those jobs are and how we will do them.

chapter 2
Seeking Out Work Opportunities

In today's working world there is no clear definition of what a job really is anymore. In the past every job came with a description, it outlined what the owner of that job was supposed to do – the roles and responsibilities that came with that particular territory. It also gave the holder of that job an identity – it was often a definer of who they were, where they fitted into society. Today the job scene is a blur. Changing demands, changing expectations and the mismatch of people skills to job needs are all part of this. Where once a person could define themselves by the job they did or the career they pursued, this is now more and more unlikely to be the case. All those predictions that we would have ten or more different jobs in our career are beginning to come true.

A decade or so ago, job-hopping was frowned on. It gave the impression you were unstable, unwilling to settle at any task for very long. Today, the opposite is true. Employers want people who have had lots of different experiences that have honed and toned up their abilities and given them a broad range of skills. As one IT manager commented, "We like people who have left us and then come back. They've learned a lot of things that make them a lot more valuable to us." And, equally, they have raised their value in the marketplace at the same time.

Fitting the culture

But still we have this seemingly unsolvable problem – would-be employees say they can't get hired, while employers complain they can't find the right people. "Globally," says labour market expert Göran Hultin, "one employer in three complains that they cannot find the skills they need." He adds, "and this isn't just about highly intelligent university graduates. In almost all labor markets, the most difficult to find professionals are the vocationally skilled ones."

Matthias Mölleney, founder of Swiss-based PeopleXpert, a training and consulting firm, agrees: "I don't think these issues are properly highlighted or understood. When we talk of talent wars the problem is that media attention focuses on the area of the battle where companies fight for top-class university graduates and the like." He continues, "The real problem does not lie there, but with the lack of professional experts like technicians, nurses and craftsmen."

It's probably more than that. Carmen Watson, Managing Director of Pertemps recruitment agency in the UK, says: "It's not actually about skills shortages – so many employers blame a dearth of talent for not being able to fill jobs – but actually, what they mean is they cannot find the right type of person to fill the role."

She suggests that "personality, attitude and cultural fit are all things that employers put first – above and beyond skills and paper qualifications." And Watson issues a warning to job seekers everywhere: "If you are fully trained, but won't 'fit in' with an organization's values, then you don't stand a chance of getting that job you covet. It is becoming critical for candidates to seek out not only the industry that suits them best, but those employers that match their way of doing things. This choosy behavior is partly due to the abundance of qualified job seekers that forces employers to look for something – other than qualifications or experience – which distinguishes the individual from the rest of the herd."

She offers this advice to would-be job seekers: "The best place to start is looking at how a company presents itself through its job adverts or website. This gives a quick snapshot of what it might be like to work there and whether it would suit your needs and personality." But Watson also says that it is the job seeker who needs to do the real soul-searching before any interview process takes place. There is a very real need for the would-be candidate to answer the following questions:

- What management culture or style gets you to perform your best?
- What are your expectations of your work colleagues?
- What is most important to you at work?

It's making sure you have a clear idea of the kind of place you want to work that will make the difference in the overall success of a career. One of the things that really turn off an employer is getting résumés from job seekers that clearly show they have not researched the company or really understood the requirements of the job being advertised (more of this later).

Having said that, employment expert Göran Hultin raises another point that employers may do well to think about: "I'd really like to know the extent to which employees feel their skills are really made use of." He continues, "I've talked with plenty of job seekers who take the attitude that this talent shortage is a myth and that employers have all the skills they need, they just don't know how to make use of it."

There's some really good common sense in this. Many employers have failed to do really accurate audits on their staff and so miss out on a lot of the talent that they already have. Worse still, many employers are making interesting mistakes when it comes to recruiting the right people. Let's consider an issue, exacerbated by current economic woes, that should be of very real concern to those seeking employment. It should also be of primary concern to employers as they search out the best talent. The issue is that sadly it would seem that employers don't always know what the best talent looks like. Worse still, many of them have such formulaic, creaky systems it's surprising they ever hire anyone.

Crowded out and bumped down

Adam Bentham is a 27-year-old communications professional based in London. He's bright, ambitious and a serial multitasker. Lately he's been considering a job change, hoping to move up the organizational ladder from his Communications Officer role with a leading aid agency, to something with more responsibilities, challenges and prospects. But, in trying to do this, Adam has hit a problem. And this problem shows two things: (1) employers don't understand much about the new digital world we now occupy and (2) don't even know the right questions to ask candidates to ensure they get the best value out of a new placement.

Here's Adam's dilemma outlined in his own words:

> I am considered generation Y, and as such I am supposedly quite desirable as an employee. One of the problems I have come across is that in the current climate, many of the senior Communications Manager roles (above Officer and below Director) are being filled with more senior people (who would normally be aiming for Director). The excuse given by employers when I miss out on these jobs is always the same, "that the organization is surprised at the level of seniority that applied for the position." So, employers are getting director-level staff at manager-level salaries and they can't say "no" to that opportunity. However, the reality is that these senior managers are then wrestling more budget from the purse-holders – persuading them with all their experience. Then they spend more than ever on costly external consultants for graphic design, social media management, branding, video editing and website development. But, these are all areas of activity and expertise that – had they appointed the "up and coming" generation Y applicant – they would have got included in the employment package in just one person – ME!

> When I was growing up at 14, 15, 16 I used to make websites in my spare time and sit at home editing videos of my friends. I used to download design programmes and spend hours drafting logos of my name just for the hell of it. I am part of a generation of highly creative and skilled individuals that's now hitting a glass ceiling after

a few years in the workplace. As a result, where the roles aren't there for us (or we are being blocked by, at first look, more experienced professionals), so many of my friends and peers are now branching out on their own as consultants – across all industries. We are not only disillusioned, we feel we are not being given the opportunities that we are skilled for.

This is a terrific and I hope eye-opening illustration of how the digitally enabled world has – in theory, if not yet always in practice – changed jobs forever. Adam is a one-man band, totally able to function at all sorts of things that would have taken an army of helpers, consultants and advisors to do in the past. And it doesn't mean that those other external suppliers don't have work – it's just done differently, that's all. Adam and those like him take care of their sphere of operations, leaving others to do the same elsewhere.

Another thing that Adam and his generation Y colleagues offer is that they don't just oversee their area of expertise. They are deeply embedded in it.

Now all it takes is to get senior managers to recognize that this is the way the world is moving forward. You see, that digital world is already changing how we think. It just needs a lot more of us to get hold of the idea and run with it. But for now, sadly, Adam and his colleagues are going to see themselves crowded out and bumped down, as those with – on the face of it – more to offer get their way.

THREE DIGITAL SOLUTIONS

The digital revolution means more than doing things differently, it means that you can do things you have never been able to do previously. It also means that there are new "jobs" that we have never seen before or old jobs fitted into totally new scenarios. Here are three examples from one crisis-hit country of why the digital world has changed us – hopefully for the better. They all took place in Haiti after the massive earthquake of January 2010.

- The earthquake knocked out fixed-line communications and disrupted transportation links. The upshot was that there was little understanding of not only where the worst damage was but also what was still functioning. In the US, at Boston University, thousands of miles away a group began to monitor cell phone calls made by Haitians to relatives and friends in the US and Canada. By doing this, the listeners were able (after just six hours of frantic activity) to build up a map that showed where there was safe water to drink, undamaged pharmacies and shops that were still open. A huge boon to rescue teams and incoming aid workers.
- One of the biggest challenges to the humanitarian aid workers trying to work in the chaos of the quake's aftermath was that Haitians speak Creole and French. Most aid workers were English speaking. Thanks to the digital workplace, translators and interpreters around the world were able to "plug" in and help out, without ever leaving their home countries. Something that would have been impossible to organize just a few years previously on any useful scale.
- Finally, the UN compound in the Haitian capital of Port au Prince got their wish. They needed a French-trained and French-speaking plumber to help rebuild the shattered infrastructure of their headquarters. The job was advertised through social networks and a Parisian plumber was duly hired and flown out to rebuild the toilet block!

How do you compete?

Adam's experiences are mirrored by those of Arnaud Houdmont, a young Belgian whose background is working in European institutions in Brussels. As with Adam Bentham, he reported that although would-be employers will meet you they usually, in the final analysis, go for the most experienced candidate. He says, "As a consequence of the financial crisis, professionals with experience can now be hired for far less (especially professionals coming from Southern Europe) and young people without experience have difficulty in competing in the current climate."

And despite everything we hear about flexible employment, Arnaud observes that "flexibility does not seem to feature high on anyone's agenda. Jobs on offer tend to be of the classic nine to five kind, with a permanent presence in the office required."

At the time of writing, Arnaud was stoically resisting applying for jobs below his experience level, but felt that this was only a matter of time as he was facing the same "crowded out and bumped down" syndrome that Adam Bentham experienced in the London job market. But there are a few things he has learned in the process and a few ideas that may be worth some employers adopting:

- Make sure your résumé is the very best you can make it. Your résumé is YOU and it needs to tell an employer who you are and why you are valuable to them. As Arnaud explains, "The first few months I did not even get invited to interviews but after having had my CV and cover letters scrutinized by two HR experts I've been invited to a considerable amount of interviews."
- Maybe employers need to be a little better at getting back to recruits. My message to employers is: you never know who you are going to miss out on. Arnaud comments, "The recruitment process tends to take place in three rounds of face-to-face interviews. This can easily take more than a month. Very often you only get answers to your applications by the time you have already forgotten you ever applied."
- Could there not be more feedback in the application process? "More often than not, the applicant is left without any idea of whether the application has been received or what the delay will be. When the application is negative, the applicant is not told and no feedback is given. It would be very useful for young people to know why their application failed, what they should improve, which skills they should acquire or polish," says Arnaud.

- Also, suggests Arnaud, "it would be ideal if applicants are given a chance to function for a day within the organization they applied to as part of the recruitment process. This would provide them with a chance to show off their skills and interact with potential future colleagues. Interviews and tests are often not sufficient to understand whether a person would be suitable for a position or not. Job descriptions also remain very vague and technical, often intimidating potential applicants."

This idea of test-driving a job has been adopted in some organizations already. As Pertemps' Carmen Watson reports, "As cultural fit grows in importance, some companies are taking a radical approach to finding the best talent. In the manufacturing sector in particular some employers are encouraging prospective candidates to take a group tour of the business to confirm if they really want to work there, before they get too far down the recruitment process."

Note: There is a great deal more practical ideas and advice on career planning and how to get hired in Chapter 5.

Think mobility

Faced with the prospect of being unable to land a job in the home country, the next step is to look across national borders. However, despite the general assumption that there are thousands of immigrants swarming all over the globe seeking out improved economic prosperity, it just isn't like that in reality. On average in the EU, less than 3 percent of a population is made up of incomers. Amazingly, as already mentioned, the vast majority of us still grow up, live and die within about 100 kilometers of our birthplace. Some say that the global communication revolution means that we can now build our careers from our own doorsteps and many are doing just that.

Indeed the FutureWork Forum/Generation Europe Foundation study on the NEXT generation discovered that young people were a lot keener to find work close to home. Not surprisingly, the most adventurous were the Italians and the Spanish, among whom youth unemployment is very high. But overall, Europe's youth are an unadventurous lot. Here's what the sample of 7,000 young people said:

Where do you look for job openings?	
Anywhere in the world	13.9%
Anywhere in the EU	20.8%
Anywhere in my country	17.7%
Regionally (inside my country)	26.8%
Locally	34.8%

Most respondents to the survey who supported the idea of cross-border working felt that it needed to be backed up by some sort of national or EU support. The creation of a Europe-wide clearing house for jobs was a popular concept. However, there were few takers for the idea that job seekers should just "go" and find out what opportunities were like in other countries.

It is perhaps useful that governments are finally coming together to tackle youth employment issues in a more proactive fashion. But it has to be done in the right way, as labor expert Göran Hultin points out:

> Labor market and employment policies do not in themselves create jobs – they seek to cushion the negative impact of a slow or declining economy. For employment to grow we need the economy to grow. If it doesn't, or if it contracts further, it does not produce jobs. So the priority of policies has to be the economy. In the absence of economic growth, the main question relevant to employment is how should we prepare for a future economic uplift? My reaction to that is – focus on the young. There is a time-bomb ticking right now, with over 50 percent youth jobless in some countries. We must train for what is needed in the job markets. To do that, we must make being a plumber or a carpenter – not just a manager or a doctor or a lawyer – a sexy career option! To do that, we need to promote and support youth entrepreneurship. Additionally, and most important, we need to put practical, active employment policies in place to get young people into work experience, even if it is subsidized.

We are back to that need for vocational skills to be promoted as much as possible. We are also back to the point that many jobs are not going to come from the big global corporations, the public sector or the large institutions. They are going to be created by individuals and small groups who – giving up on the way the job market is panning out for them – decide to go it alone: people like Adam Bentham who thinks he would have more prospects, more challenge and (he's yet to find this out) probably more fun working for himself.

Is entrepreneurism the way forward?

Adam Bentham is just one of many thinking about taking the plunge and going it alone. And as executive search consultant Anthony McAlister, who runs his global search firm in a practically virtual – and digital – space, says: "If you have a good idea start a business. There are many non-traditional ways to fund it (start with your family and friends). The experience – whatever the outcome – will be invaluable as you develop and discover what you really want to do."

McAlister suggests that if you want to go it alone you should start early – while you are still young enough to take the inevitable knocks when things go wrong. But, with a hint of cynicism born of long experience, he is also at pains to stress one very big truth that most of us fail to consider when we look at possible careers:

> The corporate dream (making it big in senior management) is just that – a dream for most of us. The reality is that very few people make it to the top and/or survive the constant restructuring and inevitable political coups … So from the outset, get real. You are most unlikely to be with any corporate organization for any length of time these days and sadly I have found that redundant senior people hardly ever recover the same remuneration and status in another organization. The real need is for everyone to ruthlessly manage their own career, get (and pay for) the best advice you can and always have a Plan B.

Taking the entrepreneurial route – effectively creating your own job – is also a preferred way forward for Atanaska Varbanova, a Romanian national working as a project director for the Brussels-based think tank and policy developer Think Young.

"More and more young people are realizing that traditional career paths are closing up and won't work for them as they did for previous generations," says Atanaska. "My feeling is that today's world is so digitized, developed and open that for many young people the traditional career path is simply not attractive anymore." She continues: "So, creating new jobs, and particularly new types of jobs, seems to be the way of the future. Here, I think, youth entrepreneurship could be a way to do it. If we really believe young people are intelligent, creative, brave, and we think they are the future, why don't we give them the opportunity to create this future?" And she adds: "Part of a possible solution could be – instead of setting up more training schemes, to think of ways to fund and support budding young entrepreneurs."

Remember Chiara Palieri, that one-woman booster of the ability of today's youth to achieve anything it wanted (Chapter 1)? Well she has some views on entrepreneurship too: "Education needs to better adapt to the reality of today's world. We must educate students while they are in school how to live with and adapt to an ever-changing market. This includes training them in life skills, social media (here's the digital emphasis again) and entrepreneurship." She ends by saying, "I think that entrepreneurship is absolutely the way forward for our generation. I strongly believe that secondary schools – and even primary education – should place more emphasis on the whole entrepreneurship concept, fostering young people to start their own businesses and working by their own rules."

Light-touch laws

There's lots of good news about start-ups as a viable alternative to just going out and trying to find a job. Governments around the globe are fast coming to the conclusion that getting people into work is not just about creating jobs and getting big companies to take people on – initiatives that often don't amount to all that much in the final analysis – but about helping people create jobs in a wide variety of ways. Interestingly, in all this there are clear winners and losers. Britain and the US are increasingly regarded as models of how to do it (the US has always been good at getting people into work – it has also, traditionally, been good at getting them out of work too, giving rise to the "hire and fire" culture). However, the UK, and especially the south of England (centered on London), has become a huge play park for entrepreneurs. Such are the so-called "light-touch" regulations of government (that make it easy to set up a business) that the southeast of the UK has been flooded with French, German, Dutch and Belgian would-be entrepreneurs.

There are good reasons for this, which bear scrutiny for anyone considering a place to start up. The UK is surrounded by countries on mainland Europe where work regulations are both restrictive and complicated. Tax incentives are few and loans just don't exist. This has led to the situation where London has the fifth largest French population and the twelfth largest German population. While many of these French and Germans work in the financial sector, increasingly it is one- and two-man start-ups that are creating these jobs. Moreover, Paris and Brussels are just two hours away by high-speed trains (that run despite fog and bad weather), meaning that people can stay in touch easily with their home cultures. At the time of writing, Amsterdam, Cologne and Frankfurt were about to be "joined" to the UK by direct train services, heralding a flurry of new arrivals. It's clear to many that if you create the right conditions to meet needs, jobs will be created.

And that is the other factor. When you get so many people in one place with the same enthusiasms it creates a buzz. The ideas flow and the whole thing just takes off. For governments seeking to foster the magic formula of how to release entrepreneurial energy into their economies, a study of London and its surroundings is a must.

Then again, we mustn't overlook that great serial-entrepreneur that is the United States of America. Start-ups there are back in fashion too – if ever they went away for very long. Observers in places such as Silicon Valley report that the number of would-be entrepreneurs meeting to discuss new business ideas in the cafes and clubs of San Francisco has doubled in recent times. Those legendary businesses of three decades ago being created on the back of a cigarette packet are now planned on a latte-stained Starbucks serviette.

Even in South Africa, entrepreneurs of all ages are picking up on the "let's create our own jobs" trend. Much of the South African urge to go it alone kicked off in the run-up to and successful hosting of the 2010 World Cup. Linked to that is a growing franchise market, with South African-created brands beginning to be seen in other geographies (think fast-food outlets such as Nandos that have taken London and New York by storm). To help get entrepreneurs launched, the South African government has a Youth Development Fund and the Black Economic Empowerment Act, which provides accreditation for black-owned small and medium-sized enterprises (SMEs).

Finally we turn to Russia, where entrepreneurism and crime seem to have merged and become indistinguishable in many places. However, with its economy stalled – except for its vast energy operations – President Putin has been forced to give an amnesty to thousands of entrepreneurs to try to get business moving again. It is estimated that upwards of 100,000 so-called "entrepreneurs" are serving prison terms for financial crimes that include fraud, embezzlement, counterfeiting and tax evasion. Putin addressed a conference in Moscow in 2013, by saying that their release would help revive the economy through "the values of economic freedom and the work and success of entrepreneurs."

Big government gets involved

But, while hot spots like London and Silicon Valley set the pace, much of what is happening in the rest of Europe – to create new jobs – is coming from the efforts of national governments and the EU to reduce the vast numbers of unemployed young people. Unfortunately, while stories about record unemployment grab the headlines, the often quiet approach by officialdom to tackling this thorny problem is seldom reported. Part of the reason is that they are working with people who need jobs in less noticeable places than trendy London, New York and Paris. However, the EU – through the European Social Fund in conjunction with member states – is trying hard and has passed a series of initiatives to create a package that guarantees every unemployed person under 25 in the EU a job, a training program or an apprenticeship.[1] While some of this can be seen as heavy-handed, unimaginative and freighted with layers of bureaucracy (but that creates jobs too, don't forget!), there are strong signs that officialdom has begun to understand how to do some of this right.

As two examples of how these initiatives are making an impact:

- In Austria, every unemployed young person is entitled to begin an apprenticeship funded by the Austrian government within three months of becoming jobless. These schemes are financed by the Austrian state at a cost of €130 million a year. However, they do work. As a result, at the end of 2012, youth employment in Austria was below 8.5 percent. What the Austrians have found is that one efficient way to help young people to take up long-term jobs is to develop individual employment strategies with them.
- In Spain, the Biscay provincial government has launched a training scheme aimed at young people in jobless households and for youth living in care homes. The local government provides these people with housing in shared flats combined with training programs. These focus on upscaling skills linked to practical, vocational education.

Let's hope the good guys continue to prevail and manage to develop a lot more practical programs that give the next generation some hope of a meaningful career. However, I'm personally not convinced

---

[1] This was subsequently amended by the European and Social Affairs Committee of the European Parliament in April 2013 to include young people under the age of 30 such as graduates and those who left the education system without any qualifications.

that the Eurocrats of the Brussels' Berlaymont are fully committed to saving Europe and the rest of the planet beyond the EU's borders. Why? Well all these initiatives were announced while I was stuck in a monster traffic jam in Brussels. The cause? Striking EU staff, protesting that they hadn't had a pay rise for two years. With generous salaries and benefits, plus a medical and pension package to die for, you have to ask if these people are in touch with reality. And if they are not, should we leave them in charge of shuffling all that paper? Yes paper. I'm not convinced that they are all that digitally savvy quite yet.

Aid is a two-way street

Of course, there are other examples where people are making a difference and providing much-needed work. One of the most heartening has come out of real crisis. As Greek unemployment spiraled in the wake of their financial crisis, a group of Greek parliamentarians got together and suggested that they find ways of getting young people into some kind of meaningful jobs. With the help of the EU they devised a scheme with the European Aid Volunteer Program and the French and Romanian Red Cross to enable out-of-work Greeks to help out in on-the-ground actions – a true case of one needy group helping out another.

More on entrepreneurs

With jobs hard to come by, and a certain amount of anecdotal evidence to suggest that the younger part of our societies don't want to go down the traditional career routes of their parents' generation, what else is happening? What other jobs are being created?

The need for people to come together socially to work is the focus of innovation hubs, which are springing up around the world. These bring people with ideas into one place where they can help each other out, pool back-office facilities and generally have a place to call home. Started in Silicon Valley some years ago, they are now dotted all over North and South America, Europe and Asia. Many think that this way of working is the future. Most importantly, it allows innovators to try out ideas without soaking up too much capital in huge fixed costs. More on this in Chapter 4.

Elsewhere, organizations such as Innovation Birmingham in the UK are encouraging small start-ups by offering them free (for a period of six months) office space, meeting rooms, phones, e-links, mentoring, and financial and marketing advice. Based in the Birmingham Science Park, they have attracted a host of start-ups all operating in the high-technology end of industry. One of the "tenants" is Soshi Games, a start-up operation begun in 2010 with just two enthusiastic people. It has now grown to a permanent payroll of 16. Its managing director and founder Cliff Dennett explains: "What is exciting is not just the creation of something from the ground up, but it is also that we are actually employing enthusiastic young people in a field that they really relate to." He continues: "Many of our employees would not have got a job if not for this. Indeed, in the early days many of our employees now on the payroll worked for free, just to get experience of the industry."

Dennett's words are endorsed by others. Starting small doesn't mean you always stay that way. These new entrepreneurs with new ideas are generating real, proper paying jobs. Indeed, in the course of researching this book, it became clear that there could well be an idea in getting established companies to help to raise the entrepreneurial banners even higher. Wouldn't it be wonderful if you could get companies – possibly by giving them a tax break to cover the costs – to hire an "entrepreneur in residence"? The idea would be to have a person (or a team) develop an idea and take it to commercial completion. At that point it could be sold off or passed on to the funding organization for further development. Then the team would start another project. This would mean that you get to help out smart young people who may not fit fully into the big corporate culture, and you get good ideas coming at you and always more in the pipeline. Maybe someone should show some entrepreneurial spirit and get it off the ground. When you consider the non-productive things that companies large and small spend their money on, it wouldn't take a lot to divert a few thousand dollars or euros to make it a reality. In fact, if you look at the overall cost of paying unemployment benefits and compare that with the cost of tax breaks to employ people, it probably works out equal.

It's not just the young who are doing this

This ability to start up new micro-businesses is not confined to the youth of today either. Thousands of people are deserting traditional company life and setting up on their own. Often they leave their employer with a service contract in their pocket to get them started. But others just want to move on to something new – or discover whether they can turn a hobby or passion into a viable job. That's the thing to consider; the word "job" doesn't necessarily cover what is happening out there. People of all ages and all levels of education are starting to think in new ways. And the digital revolution has made it all possible.

Here are some cases that I've come across in the last few months:

- A member of the managing board of one of the world's largest financial institutions took early retirement, took herself back to business school and has now transformed herself into one of the leading top-line executive coaches. She has a great and balanced lifestyle, is always busy and is in huge demand for her services. She was able to combine her interest and empathy for people with the street smarts of a corporate career, bringing her experience and knowledge to a new level of usefulness. She's a one "man" band, but she helps a lot of people find new meaning in their jobs.
- A jet-setting civil engineer, with a track record of building factories and refineries all over the world, had a health crisis. Did he hang up his hard hat? Yes he did, but he took his hobby – a love of all things food related – and turned it into a business. Working from his home initially, he built up a food product company that creates his favorite sauces and snacks from his global travels. From the outset he went after volume, selling only to food outlets, not direct to the customer, and kept to just a dozen or so products.

His engineering expertise helped him to streamline production and organize distribution. His charming wife does the selling. He now employs four local people, all of whom were unrequited job seekers until he found them.

- For 20-plus years my friend John managed a recruitment firm with branches across Belgium. Then, seemingly, disaster struck. The owner sold out and the new bosses didn't want him around. At the age of 60 John started over. British by nationality, he spoke both the French and the Dutch of his adopted homeland. He'd always been very keen on motorsport, taking part as a younger man in the Monte Carlo Rally and other races. He had contacts and he had the lingua franca of motor-racing – English. After a few hesitant months things took off. He started commentating at racing circuits, then doing the press and publicity for Dutch- and French-speaking race teams, and then acting as the local correspondent for a series of motor-racing magazines. Now 70 he has embraced his new job completely and employs two other people part-time.
- My three neighbors in my village in semi-rural Hampshire, UK, are all "refugees" from London. Each of them, wife and kids included, had a desire to swap the high-tension life of London commuting for something offering a better quality of life. Charles, an insurance executive, started up his own specialized insurance business from his home (he found he didn't like working solo so rented out some space with a few other "refugees" in the nearby town). Bill, a marketer for a global travel firm, signed up to represent a series of exclusive hotels around the globe – he does their corporate communications (yes, he's embraced digital this past decade!). He travels twice a year in a great loop around the globe. Otherwise he operates from his converted garage. My good friend Jonathan was a stressed doctor in an inner London hospital. He retrained as an acupuncturist and set up his clinic. We have a lot of people with bad backs in this part of the world and he helps them out. All three are successful, all are – more importantly – happy and fulfilled.
- Another of my friends was a high-powered corporate lawyer in Washington. A lobbyist by trade, he eventually realized that what

he was doing was perhaps making him wealthy, but it wasn't making him happy. He packed it up, to the astonishment of his fellow practice partners. What did he do? Well he swapped his three-piece suit and wingtips for chinos and loafers and picked up a brush and palette. Always good with a brushstroke, he is now exhibited by both east and west coast galleries. He has fun, smiles a lot and is now creating new jobs by starting a school for would-be painters from disadvantaged backgrounds.

Most heartening, is that all these people have brought a new vibrancy and the prospect of new jobs to the communities they have chosen to go and live in. While the world is still seen as moving from rural to urban centers, these people are reversing the trend and putting the heart back into rural communities. This is a good thing.

Now, here is one of my favorite examples of job creation.

It's not the cranes, it's the team

If you want to quickly assess the relative health of a country, city or town, there's probably no better way than to get to the highest lookout point you can find and count the number of construction cranes (there was a time not long ago when 95 percent of all the construction cranes in the world were said to be in China). While economists would most probably frown on this as an idea, for me it has always worked. A number of cranes equal lots of jobs, not just now but after the cranes have moved elsewhere and the new occupiers move into the finished buildings.

Now, let's take the crane analogy and move it to a more rural location. The villages of Kames and Tighnabruaich (meaning "house on the hill" in Scottish Gaelic) are conjoined, and at first glance sleepy little places. Bordering the mind-numbingly beautiful Kyles of Bute on Scotland's west coast, they have been a magnet for holidaymakers since Victorian times, when the rich merchants and shipbuilders of Glasgow built second homes there. Over the years these two villages have seen their fortunes fray. Much of that was down to the fact that there were so few local job opportunities that school leavers were forced to take jobs in the industrial centers of Scotland or move south to England.

However, in the last few years, that's all changed. Spurred by local tourism initiatives that have brought jobs, and the fact that the baby boomer generation are retiring and seeking out places like Kames and Tighnabruaich to put down roots, these places have found a new lease of life. Local builders, plumbers, electricians and carpenters (those jobs again!) are booked up for months as they repair, extend and weatherproof houses for the new retirees. As a result, local construction workers have developed an informal apprenticeship scheme. It works like this. The local plumber takes on the son (or daughter) of the local carpenter. He, in turn, takes on the electrician's offspring – and so on. This has had an additional benefit to the two villages. The local shinty team (a game similar to field hockey but sprinkled with liberal amounts of violence) is winning all the prizes up and down the west coast of Scotland. The reason? It can field a young, fit team, made up of those in-a-job youngsters who just a few years ago would have been forced out of their locality by the need to find work.

So, here's a thought for holidaying economists. Try out my crane theory (I think it works), but also check the local football, baseball and rugby scores too. There is a definite correlation between them and jobs – and the consequent vibrancy of the area.

JOBS FOR WOMEN IN THE WORKPLACE

Elisabeth Kelan is an associate professor at King's College London. A German national, she has researched extensively the relationship between women and the workplace. Her recent bestselling book, *Rising Stars: Developing Millennial Women as Leaders*,[2] is regarded as an insightful look into the status of women's jobs in business today. These are her views on where

---

[2] Elisabeth Kelan, *Riding Stars: Developing Millennial Women as Leaders*, Palgrave Macmillan, 2012.

the female of the species has got to in an often male-dominated working world.

Mike Johnson (MJ): There still seems to be a glass ceiling in our organizations and if you break through that glass ceiling women enter a "concrete corridor" where they are "directed" to specific job areas (HR, marketing, R&D) for the most part. Should we be looking at the careers of women from a different point of view and getting them into business in different ways?

Elisabeth Kelan (EK): Very often women are to be found in areas which do not lead to the top of organizations such as HR. The reason for this is that gender stereotypes suggest that women have strengths in certain areas such as dealing with people, which often are not regarded as skills required at the top. A way around this would be to reimagine how leaders in organizations look and behave and how a fuller skill set can be included in those perceptions, which is likely to also include so-called feminine skills. However, more importantly in the long term, we should make sure that the gender typing of skills or areas of work disappears or is, rather, so flexible that both men and women can adopt those skills.

MJ: A lot of women are giving up on mainstream corporations and going it alone. Do you think there should be more done to encourage entrepreneurship amongst women, starting at school/college/university?

EK: Encouraging entrepreneurship and looking at SMEs as employers is going to be an important source of jobs for younger people in general. In fact, there are two kinds of women entrepreneurs. First, those who gain experience in big corporations and then leave once they find the practices of those corporates out of sync with their own life cycles. Second, women from a minority background often tend to set up companies earlier in their career because many still struggle to get hired by corporates in the first place. While it is important to show that employment in your own company or in a SME is vital, this should not mean that we ignore employment in the corporate sector. It is important to show younger women the variety of job options they have. Many women entrepreneurs suffer from not asking for enough money (salary or loans) or from being denied funds by banks. There is a famous story of Anita Roddick being unable to secure start-up money from a bank when she set up the Body Shop. Instead her husband received the loan. Research indicates that this inequality in regards to female entrepreneurs still exists in so far as women entrepreneurs tend to receive lower loans. While this might be seen as prudent, this often means that female-owned companies cannot grow as fast.

MJ: Do you think that with all this youth unemployment we really do have a "lost generation" in countries like Italy, Spain, Portugal, Greece, Ireland?

EK: The current youth unemployment levels can lead to the impression that this generation is a "lost generation." The unemployment rate of young people in southern Europe and Ireland is shocking and will create social dynamite. However, other countries have found effective strategies to unfold the potential of young people. Germany has a strong system of apprenticeships that are a highly regarded way of educating younger people. Other countries such as the UK try to emulate this with limited success because the systems and structures are not in place. While this might leave us with the impression that the future for young people in the EU is bleak, I actually prefer to see the opportunities that young people in Europe have. They are also an Erasmus generation [the EU-funded, cross-border student program]. So, today young people in Europe can profit from the mobility that the European Union affords them. They can live, work and study in other countries and thereby expand their cultural horizons.

MJ: Some 20 years ago *The Economist* suggested that employers who did not have a way to access women workers were stupid, because they were squandering access to 50 percent of the world's talent. Is that still true – are we making any progress?

> EK: For most large businesses the inclusion of women is a central strategic goal. However, the expression of desire to do it and the actual reality often differ. Organizations still lose a lot of women and they need to develop ways to ensure that women can progress better within organizations. There has been some progress in including the talent that women bring, but still not enough to ensure that women's talents are fully utilized.
>
> MJ: Are you "quietly confident" that things are improving and do you have any examples that you can share?
>
> EK: I am optimistic that the nature of gender in business is changing, albeit very slowly. The biggest mistake that we can make is to presume that gender equality has been achieved. It has not, but it has shape-shifted into different forms. We need to understand how these forms work in order to dismantle them. This will take time and it will not be easy. Mainly because stereotypes are so deeply embedded in our working culture.

North to south – a trend?

One, as yet, limited phenomenon has had very little publicity: moves to shift organizations – and hence jobs – from the northern hemisphere to the south. This idea was put into practice in 2011 when a major aid organization – ActionAid – moved virtually all of its headquarters and back-office operations from London to Johannesburg. They sensibly left a large portion of their fund-raising professionals in London. Has it been a success? Human resources (HR) professional, Stanley Arumugam, was one of the architects of the move and he says that it not only worked but is being closely studied by other organizations.

"The move was always more than the physical transition from London to Johannesburg – that was successful. However, the big driver of the move was the political commitment of the organization to believing in, investing in and being governed from the south." He adds, "Now that the political signal has been communicated clearly inside and outside the organization, many other INGOs have taken note and are also considering their options too."

He continues: "Right now, Amnesty International is embarking on the same decentralized journey – establishing regional hubs outside London. However, it may be coincidental that the current chief executive of Amnesty – Salil Shetty – was the CEO of ActionAid at the time of their move!"

Arumugam thinks that this north to south model – seldom talked about – has a real future: "I believe that this trend will continue, as primarily northern-based institutions in both the for-profit and social sectors seek to connect more closely geographically with their key stakeholders."

Opportunities in China

No words on where jobs are coming from or where jobs are going to would be complete without some views on that great land of Eastern promise – China. Global labor expert and commentator Göran Hultin, who has been visiting the People's Republic for several decades, stresses that any discussion about China and jobs needs to begin with where they are right now. And in his view, stories that they will take over the world any time soon are seriously out of touch with the day-to-day reality. Hultin starts with this background, which is a necessary primer for anyone thinking about China, the global economy and jobs:

> To appreciate China's future challenges we need to keep in mind a sense of proportion. In reality, their level of economic development is still relatively low compared to the mature industrialized countries. China's average GDP per capita is about $7,600 (in Shanghai, one of the most advanced areas in the country, it hits $13,000). As you can imagine, high growth rates are easier to achieve at those low levels than at the $35–50,000 per capita levels of the Western economies. As and when the economy continues to grow and achieve higher levels of economic development the going will get more difficult, less linear and, yes, slower. Social stability will come under strain as people

expect more; businesses will need innovation, creativity and talent as they no longer can rely on low-cost labor; the education and training systems will be challenged, as it becomes increasingly clear that they do not live up to global standards and expectations.

So, where does this leave Westerners who think they may be able to improve their economic prospects by hitching onto the Chinese growth wagon? Sami Hamid spent five years working in Shanghai after graduating from a UK university. After taking a masters degree at the School for Oriental and Asian Studies (SOAS) he has returned. His on-the-ground experience makes him, in his late twenties, an old China hand. He absorbed China; he worked for Chinese companies (as their token foreigner) and learned to speak fluent Mandarin (he is also fluent in English and Spanish and has a good command of Arabic).

Asked if he would encourage others from the "West" to build their careers in China, he has this to say:

> It goes without saying all Western organizations need to be aware of China's rise to some degree. Even if they are not working directly with China they are indirectly affected by shifting economic ripples which start from China. Bearing that in mind, the young generation of upcoming Western managers would put themselves at a competitive advantage to have some exposure to China both from a professional as well as a linguist perspective. Those just starting their careers will find the first-tier cities (Beijing, Shanghai, Shenzhen) awash with internship opportunities, and if you plan your moves right, you can usually walk into a full-time job at the end of it. However, long-term success in China is most definitely tied to Mandarin-speaking proficiency. A lot of Westerners already have that as the onset of the 2008 recession saw a mass exodus of both European and US young professionals to destinations like Hong Kong, Singapore and mainland China. Adding to this, the Chinese state-run promotion to bring back Western-educated Chinese (nicknamed returning sea turtles), makes competition for full-time jobs considerable and this can only grow. With many Chinese organizations (in the main directly or indirectly state owned) now expanding abroad, Western professionals with

long-term vision would be smarter to get some mainland China experience, build up their Mandarin proficiency and then look to position themselves to these Westward-bound Chinese organizations as the crucial "must have" link to bridging the cultural and business practice gap between East and West.

Asked what skills are most in demand in China from Western people (what skills and attributes the Chinese don't have themselves), Sami Hamid says:

Creativity and innovation are still sorely lacking in China. This has its roots in an education system which follows the strong Confucian values of "do not question your teacher," meaning it is heavily geared towards rote learning without any real critical thinking involved. This means many graduates, even at university level, are not prepared with the necessary skills to be innovative or creative when joining the workforce. There are two camps of thought in regards to China's future. Some believe the huge infrastructure and investment China is making into its R&D and high-tech fields will see it emerge as a technological leader in the near future, pioneering the way in new innovative products and industries (similar to the story of Japan in the 1970s and 80s). While others believe the state push is not enough and China will continue to simply copy developed Western technologies and adapt them to the Chinese market. Either way, there is a huge demand for foreign R&D and high-tech industries to enter China's marketplace so that the Chinese can learn how to develop their own domestic industry.

With a lot of the focus around the globe on many of tomorrow's jobs coming from start-ups and other entrepreneurial activity, what is happening in China? What looks like happening is that, again, the state is making much of the running. The Chinese government realizes that decades of communism have not exactly encouraged a nation of entrepreneurs – so they are trying to change that in a big way. While accurate numbers are hard to come by, reports from China suggest that the state is planning to sponsor the creation of upwards of 500,000 entrepreneurs in the next five or six years. Already they are organizing "how to run a business" classes in many cities, with the simple idea of getting many people to be their own boss. Again, for a huge (perhaps better to say vast) number of people, the concept of what a job is, is changing forever.

The status of a job

Then, of course, there's the issue of a particular job's status, especially how it is regarded in a society. For example, such are the complications to getting a commercial driver's licence – and the necessary insurance – in countries such as China, that this type of job has a high status. Equally, across most of Asia aid workers are looked down on as filling second-rate jobs. However, in Africa, aid workers are very often at the top end of the professions (you can build a very satisfactory career out of being an aid worker there). But then again, even if the job is accorded high status, there is still a distinct pecking order. Those who work for small aid agencies are at the bottom, and status increases dependent on how globally important your choice of employer is. The top status is always reserved for those who get to work for the UN agencies. They pay – literally – top dollar. In aid organization terms, if you get a job with the UN you really can claim to be a "top banana."

Creating a logjam of talent

There is a lot in this chapter about start-ups, entrepreneurs and people doing what they want rather than what they were originally trained or told to do. That's going to continue. As I travel I notice that there are a massive number of people in their 60s and 70s refusing to retire. Are they blocking up the system, not giving way to the next generation, hogging much-needed jobs? Personally, I don't think so. As people live longer and they remain active they want to continue making a contribution to the lives of others and keeping themselves "alive" at the same time. The UK government – and I doubt it is the only one – evince surprise that there are now more than a million people over retirement age (65) still working. It keeps being a major news item. While some of them clearly have to continue working for straightforward economic reasons, there are many who do it for the fun of it. That's not going to go away.

All I would suggest is that these bright "oldies" should not be complained about – they should be celebrated and rewarded. Why? Because, through their enthusiasm, they can mentor and teach the next generations. They can be the voice of experience that many seeking out a job for the first time could use as a place for advice.

Some years ago a friend of mine told me that he thought that this age we live in was the best ever for a very simple reason. We were perhaps the very first generation that – due to longer lifespans – had both our parents and our grandparents alive as we grew up. "Imagine how lucky we are to be able to learn from not one, but two generations," he enthused. Well, he was right. And we need to use that gift of longer lives to help next generations make it in their chosen job. What has been proven is that there is no limit to the jobs we can do, how, where, why, when we do them and for how long.

chapter 3

People, Positions and Places

We're teetering on the abyss of mass unemployment, right? Not really. It depends who you are, what you can do and where you live. Consider this: according to the European Union, member states require something in the region of 700,000 computer literate workers by 2015. These people – to quote a report from the Brussels-based lobby group Think Young,[1] – "appear to be missing." The word "missing" is a euphemism for "shortage." Nobody worked out ahead of time that these people might be needed in this digital world of ours and consequently they never got trained. It's interesting to talk with IT professionals who'll tell you ruefully that even today – when the computer, the tablet and the iPhone are ubiquitous bits of kit – there is very little computer programming taught in schools. All the majority of school and college leavers seem capable of doing is downloading apps and using already programmed software.

Skills Provision, a recruitment firm founded in the UK, notes that skills shortages are not unusual – they're just getting worse. And according to them, it is a combination of "an ageing population, increased baby boomer retirement, misdirected education policies, technology impact

---

[1] "Youth Attitudes to the Job Market: Overcoming the Skills Mismatch," Think Young, 2013.

and social change that are the drivers." In other words, everyone is to blame one way or another. But what Skills Provision and other people experts such as Manpower Inc point out is that the jobs in short supply are the basic ones. Sure we may be a few rocket scientists short, but that is not supercritical – because we don't need that many. But when you consider that even the most modest uptick in a nation's economy can drive a need for a particular job category, then you've got to take notice. Many of these are not superstar jobs, just the run-of-the-mill employment. A good example is that of janitors. The US Bureau of Statistics (those demographic professionals who predict who we need, where and when) reckons that in America alone there are going to be a quarter of a million new janitorial positions to fill by 2020.

Back at Skills Provision, they reckon that when looking at the job skills in short supply, the top ten industries throughout 2013 and 2014 would be:[2]

1. IT specialists: we have already mentioned those 700,000 "missing" in Europe.
2. Healthcare: ageing populations the world over mean that there is an ever-increasing need for doctors, nurses and other health specialists.
3. Engineering: lots of reports of process engineers in short supply the world over.
4. Basic trade skills: plumbers, plasterers, bricklayers, electricians, roofers. There just never seems to be enough of them. And with not just ageing populations, but shrinking ones too (at the youth end of things), there just won't be enough to go around to meet demand.
5. Mechanics: booming new markets such as Africa, Asia and South America soak up talent in this area if it is prepared to travel.
6. Education: this sector is still growing rapidly, especially as Asia and Africa seek to be educated in the West.

---

[2] "Top 10 International Skill Shortage Predictions for 2013," Skills Provision Limited.

7. Natural resources: with an emphasis on real workers, not managers.
8. Aviation: pilots and skilled ground staff. Focus moves from Europe and North America to other regions as they expand economically.
9. Training and development: huge needs to develop people more and to upskill those who need it.
10. Chefs and other hospitality professionals. Skills Provision says that "from Australia to Canada there is a huge shortage of top class chefs."

THE BEST-PAID JOB

Probably the best-paying chef jobs are to be found in extreme places (cooking for scientists in Antarctica pays very well, as does cooking on deep-sea oil rigs). The other great job for chefs is on submarines. The Australian Navy pays around US$200,000 for a chef – more than a junior admiral gets. It takes the submarine sandwich to new depths – doesn't it?

These skill and job shortages are mirrored, at least in part, by Manpower's own research. However, they place "Skilled Trade Workers" firmly at the top of their hard-to-recruit list, saying that vocational professionals are the lifeblood of all kinds of operations just about anywhere around the globe.

If you're in the US and you want to know what to study, train and develop for, the US Bureau of Labor Statistics can help out – big time. This is their list of top jobs for 2012, which projects the number of expected openings in trades or professions until 2020.

Trades and professions most in demand 2012 to 2020:

1. Dentist
2. Registered Nurse: huge growth in the healthcare industry driven by an ageing population
3. Pharmacist
4. Computer Systems Analyst
5. Physician

6. Database Administrator
7. Software Developer
8. Physical Therapist
9. Web Developer
10. Dental Hygienist
11. Occupational Therapist
12. Vet
13. Computer Programmer
14. School Psychologist
15. Physical Therapist Assistant
16. Interpreter/Translator
17. Mechanical Engineer
18. Veterinary Technologist
19. Epidemiologist
20. IT Manager

The least-favored job – out of the 100 listed – was telemarketer. Now why would that be?

Tough to fill

Not only are these jobs in demand – and getting more so every day – they are getting tougher and tougher to fill. According to Manpower's research, the problem is acute and worldwide: "In India and Brazil, two of the world's fastest growing economies, 48 percent and 71 percent of employers are having trouble filling positions. In the US and Australia, two strong and mature economies, 49 percent and 50 percent of employers cannot find the right talent to help grow their businesses." Note the phrase "right talent" here. That is the crux of the matter. There are plenty of warm, unemployed bodies around. But they're not qualified to do the jobs on offer in today's workplace, as we saw earlier in the Jaguar Land Rover need for 1,700 new jobs.

Manpower has more to say on this, and it makes disturbing reading: "Even in Europe, where a highly educated workforce and chronically high unemployment makes finding talent relatively easy, some employers are having trouble. In Germany, 42 percent of employers report difficulties finding good candidates. In Japan, the world's third largest economy, an astounding 81 percent of employers indicate that finding qualified hires is a problem."

The German figure is perhaps the most worrying, because they and near neighbors Austria and Switzerland have been at great pains to make sure they have the people they need. As Swiss-based PeopleXpert founder Matthias Mölleney comments, "If we look at figures for youth employment, we see that Germany, Austria and Switzerland are the best three countries. Coincidently, these are the three countries which have followed a dual professional training model." He explains that " after nine or ten years of school, kids start an apprenticeship in any profession (carpenter, clerk etc.). And, in parallel to this apprenticeship, they go to a special school (mandatory) once a week. This twin track model prepares them for both a professional career after the apprenticeship and allows them to continue their education up to the level of university."

Based on what Mölleney says, you'd think that Germany would be getting it right – but it isn't. And the problem is just as bad elsewhere. Across Asia-Pacific, nearly half of all employers in Australia, New Zealand and Taiwan can't find the right talent.

AID SECTOR AS A VIABLE CAREER

Another area of "new" jobs is the international aid and development sector (often referred to as the third sector. The question is, can you make a successful and reasonably well-rewarded career whilst helping people around the globe recover from war, famine and other disasters?

Ben Emmens is a freelance consultant in the aid sector. Until recently he was the director of HR programs at the aid agency People In Aid. His view is that:

> Yes, careers can be made despite the often held view that it's an industry supporting an industry. And neither is it a career where one can get rich; those days are over. Having said that, certainly UN roles and jobs with some key aid donors and the big

foundations (think Clinton and Gates Foundations) will pay well, certainly a good market rate that you'd find in the for-profit sector. Getting your foot in the door isn't always easy. When you are young, it's usually with a small NGO [non-governmental organization]. Then with more experience other opportunities open up, especially if you have transferable skills. Prospective candidates for these kinds of careers should be looking at the Red Cross Code of Conduct to get some ideas of the values and principles involved. Also, it's good to remember that international development is often considered separately from civil society/voluntary sector opportunities ... as for key skills it's more a question of being good at your discipline and getting a lot of experience. Don't forget we are now looking at the coming of age for what is, in total, a trillion-dollar sector. New actors such as the military, private sector and entrepreneurs (e.g. Toms Shoes[3]) mean lots of change and challenge. There's always been a real lack of formal career paths – and recognition of prior experience, which needs to change. Good places to start looking are organizations like Save the Children and Catholic Relief Services, with graduate recruitment schemes and innovative internships. Several organizations maintain close links with some universities.

Hazel Douglas, the founder of Oxford HR, a specialist recruiter in the third sector, agrees with Emmens' view that you can build a career in the aid agency world, but tempers it with a note of caution: "Yes, we are seeing better salaries and conditions attracting people who wouldn't have come to the sector before now. However, I think that part of it is that there are fewer jobs in the private sector at the moment – so competition is greater."

Douglas adds, "Certainly jobs in this sector are not as bad as they used to be. However, to make a successful transition from for-profit to non-profit a really good onboarding program is vital – we just do things differently."

But Douglas is careful not to talk up the aid sector too much: "The problem at present is that we are rushing headlong into a tick-box culture (driven by government regulations) and this is a shame, as it puts people off joining."

---

[3] Toms is a for-profit company based in Santa Monica, California, which operates the non-profit subsidiary, Friends of Toms.

Heard about hysteresis?

In fact the situation is so bad, that Manpower thinks that many employers have just given up and are working with the idea that there will always be talent shortages – it's just the way things are. They feel that a long-term crisis, after a period of time, isn't a crisis anymore, it is just the status quo. Manpower suggests that "the US is in danger of falling into what economists call hysteresis in the job market, which is when those long-term unemployed (around 13 million in the US) become permanently unemployed because of a variety of factors: employer bias against the unemployed; the erosion of job skills, caused by being away from work; and a loss of confidence among the unemployed because they can't find work."

Manpower sees this state of affairs as a troubling one: "In Europe in the 1980s, governments did little when unemployment increased and, after enough people had been unemployed for enough time, unemployment rates stayed stubbornly near 10 percent because of hysteresis in the job market." They continue, "The prescriptions to combat hysteresis in the job market are well known: subsidized job-sharing and more aggressive monetary and fiscal policy among them." They then ask the key question, and provide the answer: "Why isn't there more urgency to deal with the problem? Because we are starting to get used to it."

Manpower does praise some employers who are trying to fight these talent shortages – not with government help but on their own: "One in four employers provides more training to existing employees and about one in eight expands the search for candidates outside their immediate geographic region. Roughly the same number appoints candidates to roles they aren't quite qualified for, but can learn to grow into. All are effective ways of dealing with talent shortages."

Certainly, an increasing number of employers are saying that they can't find the right people. And there is a good case to be made – as we have already seen – that part of the problem begins with individuals being unaware of what types of jobs are in demand and training for these. As the Think Young study "Youth Attitudes to the Job Market" discovered (page 58), "young people regularly overlook the demands of the labor market when making educational choices – often pursuing career goals based upon personal interests and cultural influences." The report states: "This indicates a failure within the education systems and of enterprises to effectively signal the required skills and educate students to fill these voids in the market."

The Think Young report also says that young people need to know more about what's available: "Many of the programs offered by the EU, that aim to increase participants' career prospects are largely unknown, or are not used by a vast majority of young individuals and business professionals." This is a key point. When a group of young European graduates were questioned about EU programs that exist to help them, the Erasmus program was well known and used, but none or very few had heard of other initiatives: Comenius, Edulink, Erasmus Mundus, Erasmus for Entrepreneurs, Youth in Action and External Cooperation would seem to be operating under deep cover. Never mind those graduates, have you heard of any of these programs that purport to help young people into the right kind of trades and professions?

Even if job seekers do get to the starting gate, and send out applications, industry reports say that these are often either poorly targeted or ill thought out. Think Young asked the views of several major employers about their experiences with first-time job candidates – the responses were not encouraging. Here's part of their report:

> All respondents pointed out that candidates too often lack not only hard skills, but also soft skills. For example most candidates applying for sales positions have never experienced a real negotiation. In another case the recruiter reported that some candidates lacked confidence with office tools such as Microsoft Word or Excel, or tended to make major mistakes in daily routines such as sending informal emails to the chief executive or hitting the "Reply to All" button!
>
> For many of those asked about their experiences, hard skills were the issue. Many candidates lacked mathematical and technical skills and knowledge was very general. Many new engineers have often only

applied hard sciences at a theoretical level and have never experienced applications at an operational level. Some young people do not realistically understand what working life really means, as it appears they live in a theoretical, sheltered bubble.

One of the key and influential factors affecting skill mismatch is attitude. Many CVs are not well structured, giving off the perception that while the candidate has many technical skills he or she is not willing to commit seriously. In one example, the expert described a CV in which the candidate was listening to music in the attached picture!

LET THE GAMES BEGIN

Talk about computer games and an image of an overweight adolescent, lying prone on a couch with a console in his hand, springs quickly to mind. But the fact is that most games developers I have met may have that prerequisite geeky air about them, but they look more in need of a good meal than anything – the product of long hours of coding, I gather!

Games development is very much a male preserve, but one of the leading designers in the UK is Helen Routledge, Systems Design Manager of Totem Learning in Coventry,[4] who says that the industry is crying out for good people but that, until recently, programming has not been a subject widely taught in schools. All this, however, is in the process of changing.

Asked if schools/colleges are doing enough for (or are even aware of) the job potential in the games industry, she explains: "There are definitely some innovators in the education space who recognize the potential of the games sector as a future employer. But overall the focus on programming, ICT skills and creative skills historically has been lacking, which, given our strong IT heritage in the UK, is pretty appalling."

But, she enthuses, things are getting better: "Until recently, for the majority of students, ICT revolved around how to use Excel

---

[4] Coventry, together with Birmingham and the rest of the Midlands in the UK, is a hotbed of gaming firms and independent, freelance programmers.

and PowerPoint in their ICT lessons – focused on learning how to USE software programs rather than understand any of the underlying computer science. Programming has only recently (Sept 2012) become part of the ICT curriculum (now renamed as computer science), so every child in the UK will be given an opportunity to learn the foundational principles of computer science.

"Also, attitudes are changing and computer science is now being seen as a STEM subject – having strong links with maths, engineering and science – and there's a lot of attention and funding for STEM subjects at the moment. The Computing at School Working Group hint at computer science being as important to learn as numeracy and literacy."

Routledge continues, "At Totem Learning, we try to do what we can to encourage people to learn more about the industry. We offer work experience placements to young people to give them a taste for the industry, but those we take on are often already aware of the opportunities."

Just to give some idea of the numbers of people employed in the games sector, according to the third annual Game Developer Census by Game Developer Research (2011), which covers North American game companies:

- Canada now employs 12,480 people in the games industry.
- In 2008, Canada employed 9,500 people in the games industry.
- California has 20,815 developers (46 percent of the US total).
- Washington has over 4,500 games industry employees.
- Texas has over 2,600 games industry employees.
- Game tools companies, game contracting/services companies, external PR, marketing, legal and other business services, and liaison or licensing divisions at larger media companies are not included in the census; however, Game Developer Research estimates this number at around 20,000 across North America.

Oh, and yes, it really is true, computer geeks ARE boys. According to the stats, 87 percent of workers in the games industry are guys.

The computer as recruiter

Of course, the alternative to getting frustrated by the relative merits of a résumé, is to let the digital world do it for you. Increasingly, employers faced with having to recruit many people (particularly at the low-wage end of the reward spectrum) are turning to what is termed as "machine-readable" software.

Corporate giant Xerox – the one-time photocopier producer that has a stated ambition to be one of the world's largest outsourcing companies (running customer service centers, handling health claims and processing credit card data) – is one of the many companies going down the computerized résumé reader route. Most of the need has been driven by the fact that Xerox and companies like them have major levels of staff attrition, and need to hire thousands of new people each year. At Xerox, the vice president for recruitment, Teri Morse, reports that because of high attrition rates they will have to replace around 20,000 of their workforce of 50,000 plus service agents each year. Morse explains that employees who stay for less than six months cause a loss, due to the costs of training them. So, getting a better understanding of who people are – before they get hired – can make a huge difference in how long employees stay in the job. This is crucial to whether businesses make a loss or a profit.

The data Xerox gathers include personal profiles and how far the candidate would have to travel to work – a short commute is a must as it means a person is less likely to quit before the company can recoup its cost to train them.

Other organizations are getting in on the act as well. One of the best known examples of trying to hire, reward and fire by the numbers is Google (whose human resources department is called "People Operations"). They have turned hiring into a huge computer game project, using computer models to determine how many times each candidate should be interviewed, how big the wage increases should be and nearly every other personnel decision.

Since the company started using the machine-readable system, Xerox says that employees stick on the job longer and their productivity improves. And there's another advantage too. They are able to broaden the base of people they consider to hire for hourly jobs, including those who have been unemployed for long periods. Morse says that the company won't even begin to look at résumés of candidates who score in the "red" category of the automated assessment process. "Individuals who test strongly perform better and survive longer," she says. At the beginning, while testing the system, Xerox still hired against the advice of the data. It isn't like that anymore. "People who do poorly in the tests, we no longer hire," says Morse.

Gray hair can be good

One group that probably wouldn't get past the first question of a machine-readable application is the older members of the workforce. But in a world where accusations of ageism are often thrown about, some, at least, are fighting back and making a virtue out of their age – and the attendant experience it brings.

In Dallas, Texas, two public relations industry veterans, Reg Rowe and Michelle Metzger, have launched GrayHairPR, a virtual agency that taps into the extensive experience and expertise of other well-seasoned PR professionals around the country. The idea is that the network can provide superior services to CEOs who are tired of dealing with youngsters that GrayHairPR says would "rather tweet than meet."

"The inconvenient truth about today's young PR practitioners," says Rowe, "is that many are poor writers and don't understand that the best social media outreach is practiced face-to-face. Simply put, they can text and tweet, but they can't write or meet!"

"Seasoned PR veterans have earned their gray hair taking critical reporter calls at 3 a.m. or feeding talking points to CEOs seconds before a high-stakes interview," says Metzger. But they aren't avoiding the new digital age either. GrayHairPR will be using the latest technology tools by feeding meaningful content through a company social media channel and will launch a proprietary digital thought-leader tool.

Planning for an ageing workforce

However, not everyone is eager to write off the older members of the workforce and for good reason. With declining birth rates older workers will soon be a key part of any organization's payroll – a fact not lost on German automaker BMW. They have been experimenting with ideas aimed at making sure they embrace the need for older workers on their production lines.

In a series of "live" experiments, BMW staffed a production line in one of its Bavarian manufacturing plants with a group of workers with an average age of 47 years – that's eight years older than the usual make-up of an assembly team.

The project, called "Heute für Morgen" (Today for Tomorrow) was about making sure BMW had the right people, equipped with the right tools, ten years down the road, and the 47-year-olds represented the older workforce that the company expects to employ in the future.

BMW have reported that the "oldie" production line was a great success. The 42-member assembly team created 70 changes in the way they worked. These included the acquisition of specially designed ergonomic chairs and magnifying lenses, to help minimize eyestrain. Best of all, the group increased productivity by 7 percent, making them as productive as the lines composed of younger workers.

Others are taking this future impact of an ageing workforce seriously too – and it isn't all about high technology either. At the UK's Loughborough University, they have spent four years studying the impact of an ageing workforce in a project called "Working Late."

One of their key findings was that physical activity is very important. "Sitting at a desk all day isn't a good idea," explained Cheryl Haslam, who led the study. "We had a project called 'Walking Lunch' where we put a large map on the office wall and encouraged people to go out for a walk rather than sit inside and eat a sandwich. We asked them to take a picture on their cell phone of things they'd seen that might interest others and then installed special printers in the office that people could use with their smartphones. They printed the photo and put it on the map. They were sharing local knowledge and feeling a lot more refreshed at the same time."

What's the news on expatriates?

Time was, when being an expatriate – sent out from your home country or your firm's headquarters to organize a local office – was the dream of many an ambitious career-climbing executive. That phrase, "I'm from HQ and I'm here to help you," used to strike either fear or amusement into the hearts of the locals – depending on the person that London, New York or Frankfurt had sent.

But the world has got smaller, budgets have got tighter and the big houses, servants and chauffeur-driven cars for "our man in Malaya, Hong Kong or Africa" went the way of suits and ties and the telegram. So what's life like for an expatriate today? Malcolm Johnson is a leading figure in the expatriation world and is a founder of Atlas Consulting, a Brussels-based firm that specializes in tracking expatriate activity and the working conditions and perks that expatriates get for many of the world's largest corporations.

Are people today still as likely to cross borders in pursuit of career goals?

According to Johnson:

> Yes, they are. Globalization demands and needs expatriates and, although the style is changing, the numbers continue to increase year on year. But there are challenges. It is no longer that old-fashioned stereotype of a man with non-working wife and two kids to move. It may be a young (female) bank executive who insists that she takes her child with her to China, and the au pair comes too. And if her organization can't make that happen then she's not going. It may be a family which involves live-in grandparents and if the assignee goes it is him/her and the kids and the parents – all three generations …

Companies are responding to the need for expats – and the ever-increasing cost of expats – by juggling with policies and introducing new lower-cost expatriation plans. The classic expatriate balance sheet works well but is expensive. So we see the use of adapted balance sheets (with, for example, fewer benefits being offered to assignees going on developmental assignments), or a local-plus contract (where the expat gets a percentage more than a local hire until they have adapted to the new conditions). Other recent innovations include a "backpacker" contract for someone who "volunteers" to go abroad and will live with relatives or friends. Also, in terms of nationality, increasing globalization has made itself felt and global mobility programs typically involve a lot more "home" countries than in the past. I think it fair to say that as the Westerners are less easily expatriated, often because of dual career issues (where either the husband or wife don't want to leave for their own career reasons), other nationalities are stepping in. East and South Europeans and Indians now make up a significant number of the world expatriate community.

And which expatriates are in the greatest demand? Johnson doesn't hesitate in answering, "Engineers and more engineers! Followed by production experts and research talent, especially in the pharma industry."

THE MIDDLE EAST WORKPLACE

The Middle East is a highly diverse region, with a real economic mix of countries, some oil rich, others relatively impoverished. But what is the employment outlook like across the region? Labeed Hamid is the president and founder of the Middle East Management and Research Center based in Dubai. He has observed the Middle East's challenges for over four decades. So, what are the headlines for the region when it comes to employment?[5]

"There are of course a lot of differences between countries," explains Hamid. "High populated countries such as Egypt have

---

[5] Labeed Hamid, of the Middle East Management and Research Center, gave this interview in June 2013.

suffered for many years from high unemployment even though young Egyptians have been the source of skilled and unskilled human resources for the low populated oil rich countries of the Gulf. Teachers, doctors and managers have been flocking to the Gulf countries to fill jobs created by the oil booms of the 1960s and 70s and have become an integral part of the economic structure. Egypt has also been a good source of unskilled labor throughout the Middle East, although they have been vulnerable to political changes and unstable economic climate caused by the Arab Spring and other major events such as the two Gulf wars."

And what of job prospects? "Unemployment of young Arabs is a somewhat different phenomenon than European youth unemployment," says Hamid. "Young Arabs are not tempted by work in menial jobs. They focus on government jobs which provide security, continuity and prestige among their peers and family. This is an acute problem throughout the Arab world and has historical and cultural roots.

"This, of course, led to importing unskilled labor for all economic sectors. Several hundred thousand Filipino workers have been imported to fill demand for domestic jobs (maids and cleaners), bus drivers and junior secretaries. Several thousand workers from Pakistan and Afghanistan work as building laborers, gardeners and taxi drivers. Thousands of Indians are working in the Arab World in all types of jobs. These are jobs that the young Arab does not want to do and would rather stay unemployed. As long as this mentality prevails, and I see little sign of this changing, we will have young people waiting for government job vacancies and we will continue to import labor from the rest of the world."

Asked to predict future trends, Hamid is cautious in his response:

> *Projects to alleviate unemployment are lacking. Business schools and MBA degrees are being offered all over the Middle East. Almost every prestigious American, Australian and Canadian university has a joint venture or a "campus" in the Arab world. But*

> these universities are conferring highly prestigious degrees to ambitious young Arabs who will be looking for highly paid jobs in one of the government enterprises. These institutions are not graduating entrepreneurs, who will start businesses and create jobs and employment. Teaching entrepreneurship is seriously lacking in our education of the future Arab generation. There are hundreds of "Leadership" seminars and courses and academies, but hardly any that educate and help young people in how to start small businesses. Online education is new and mostly developed by Western educational institutions with little or no adaptation to the local environment. They are offered in English, which places a limit to the number of people that can use them It's not surprising that unemployment in the region has fueled the past two years of violent uprising and what was called the Arab Spring. A frustrated young generation growing up in one of the richest regions in the world cannot understand their leaders and government economic and political policies. These policies have not been successful in fostering sustainable economic prosperity, nor have they brought political stability to the region. The religious divide is worse now than 50 years ago; the conflict with Israel is over 65 years old and no solution is in sight; fundamentalism and extremism are thriving and threatening to swamp the voices of reason and moderation.

Asked about investment opportunities that create jobs, Hamid commented:

> Investors in the region have been active for many years. Most international oil companies have joint ventures in the Middle East. The banking sector has been growing and most international banks have branches in the region. Hotel chains are spread around the Arab World. These business ventures have employed a cross-section of the young population both as managers and workers. Government projects in the gas and chemical industry have created hundreds of jobs in the Gulf. The explosion of the telecommunication industry has also created an active employer in recent years. There is still much more room for outside investors such as in the relatively young tourist sector in countries slowly opening up to tourists such as Iraq, the UAE and Oman. However, regional instability will always remain a deterrent for investors. It is fair to conclude that the region with its vast wealth has the potential of keeping everyone employed and creating

> a prosperous and highly educated society that can rival any advanced Western country today. But the reality of potential instability remains high. This reality is also robbing the region of a highly educated young generation who – whenever possible – emigrate and settle around the world wherever they can improve their economic situation and where they can raise their families in a stable and stress-free environment. Thousands of young graduates from the Middle East can be found today holding responsible jobs in Europe, America and Australia. Their countries have lost them forever and will continue to lose many more unless fundamental changes take place in the region to provide the young emerging generation with a similar quality of life that exists in the developed world.

A word about places

There is absolutely no doubt that talent gravitates to places where other like-minded individuals congregate. Financial experts colonize New York, London, Frankfurt, Zurich and Hong Kong; pharmaceutical professionals head for New England and Switzerland where the great research laboratories are located. Creative types such as advertising executives and media specialists head to Los Angles, New York, London and Amsterdam. All of these people know that these places offer the very best jobs, the biggest challenges and – of course – the biggest pay checks.

Think of it this way. If you are an organization that wants to get into the big time in your industry, you won't achieve that in some semi-rural backwater. The reason? You'll never attract the people you need to make your organization grow and prosper.

If you are an individual, the same applies. You need to be a part of the heady mix that means you meet, greet and hang out with people who you can learn from, do business with and develop your skills through.

Innovative cities (and the regions around them) feed on themselves and act as beacons of light, giant troughs of talent that more and more people want a piece of. Sure, there may come a time when you are well established in your chosen profession and you can choose not to play inside the honey pot of talent every working day. But as you leave and take your well-earned cash with you, others will be lining up to take your place.

These locations work, not because some PR person said we should be excited about a place, but because they serve a purpose – they provide a profession, or professions, with access to all they need both when they are working and when they are playing.

Everyone needs to realize that:

- People flock to the best locations for their talent – where they can be who they want to be.
- Being amongst the herd makes changing jobs or getting freelance work easy.
- You need to watch the demographics – needs and places change as people age.
- If you get it wrong, it's going to hurt hard. That's why Shanghai and Beijing are full of young professionals. The mature talent – the ones with families and a lifestyle all worked out – prefer Australia, the US, the UK and Switzerland. Those seeking out talent need to remember that.

A tale of eight cities

To give you some idea of how this city-attraction thing works, let's look at eight different global cities:

- Los Angeles: Center of the global entertainment industry, it naturally attracts the beautiful and the bright wheelers and dealers and has done so for over a century. Despite California's fiscal woes, it shows no sign of pulling down its shingle as the fun-house of the planet.
- San Francisco: LA's northern – and some would say more cerebral and liberal – neighbor. Where the digital world's super geeks do business and party all at the same time.

- New York: As the song says, "If I can make it there, I'll make it anywhere." How true, but all those Wall Street bankers, Park Avenue lawyers and admen have no plans to go anywhere else. Also a glowing beacon of publishing, new media and the countercultures. Finally, it's always been hugely cosmopolitan and continues to be so, building on that mix of people to create a magical cultural experience.
- Zurich and Geneva: Both five-star *boutique-style* cities. Terrific locations. Great education, healthcare and lifestyle; lakes, mountains and the Mediterranean just hours away. Access to huge talent pools. Low taxation and a business-minded government. Add in sleepy Basel if you are a pharma-research whizz.
- Hong Kong: A magnet for expatriates wanting a springboard to mainland China. Low taxes, low cost of living, easy to start up a business.
- Amsterdam: Just very cool and very creative. Great liveability and renowned Dutch liberal attitudes. First openly "gay" city on the planet.
- London: The most cosmopolitan city in the world. Fifth largest French population, twelfth largest German population. Global epicenter of finance, arts, new media. Massive cross-pollination of talent. Easy to start a business and low taxes. Much less bureaucracy than the rest of red-tape Europe.

SOUKTEL – A GREAT IDEA

One of the biggest problems about jobs is that often the people who need them most don't know that someone is looking to hire (think about that quote of Charles Dickens). Now in the Middle East and Africa a new movement has started that takes an age-old need (a job) and links it to modern technology. Souktel is a mix of the traditional Arabic word "souk," meaning market, and "tel" – we know what that means. Put them together and you have a service to help job seekers find work easily and quickly, using SMS and voice menu technology as the basis. Founded by Palestinian, Canadian and American graduate fellows at Harvard University and MIT, what Souktel has done is tap into the explosion in cell phone ownership in low-income countries (in Kenya cell phone ownership has risen by 180 percent since 2011; in Palestine 80 percent of the youth own cell phones; in Bangladesh there are 30 cell phones for each web user).

Since its beginning in 2006, Souktel has seen the number of users spiral ever upward. The USP (unique selling proposition) is that you only need a mobile, not an expensive weblink. And it means that users can send thousands of messages for very little cost, reaching out to rural communities that have little access to infrastructure. Its ability as a recruiting format has brought thousands of jobs to people who otherwise would be unemployed.

And here's another one – Medellín

Yes, that Colombian city, once famous for being the murder capital of the world,[6] has been reformed since the 1990s when cocaine king Pablo Escobar ruled the streets. Since then the murder rate has fallen more than 80 percent and in 2013 Medellín was named the "World's Most Innovative City."

Known by Colombians as "the City of Eternal Spring," Medellín was chosen for its progress, potential, rich culture and impressive strides in urban development. The city has built public libraries, parks, schools in poor hillside neighborhoods and constructed a series of transportation links from these areas to its commercial and industrial centers. Links include a metro cable car system and huge "travelator" escalators up steep hills, dramatically reducing commuting times and improving access for everyone, which has spurred private investment and promoted social equality.

The reinvention of Medellín is a huge success story. Engineering firms designed public buildings for free and nine of the city's largest firms funded a new science museum. In addition it is one of the few cities

---

[6] A murder rate of 380 per 100,000 people compared with the current murder capital title-holder San Pedro Sula in Honduras with a rate of 169 per 100,000 in 2012.

to introduce participatory budgeting, which allows citizens to define priorities and allocate a portion of the municipal budget. Community organizations, health centers and youth groups have formed, empowering citizens to declare ownership of their neighborhoods.

As a result, talent is flocking to Colombia's second city. It's the place to be.

Interestingly enough, there were two other awards made. Tel Aviv was named "Technology" city of the year and New York was named "Liveability" city.

A JOB TO MAKE THEM CRY

Is this the ultimate job? Totem Learning's Helen Routledge says that there is an ultimate goal in the gaming industry: "creating a game that makes people cry." So far no one has been able to make that happen, but it is regarded as the Holy Grail of gaming. Imagine having that on your résumé or business card ... John Smith, Cry Maker.

You just know it's going to happen, don't you?

Getting it wrong

Of course, not everyone appreciates the need to give talent the environment to thrive. Some firms get it badly wrong. The stories that follow both involve two of our chosen talent-magnet cities mentioned previously.

The first is London, where the global publishing giant Pearson has its headquarters. A mile or so away from Pearson's HQ they had a significant number of their publishers and editors working on the fringes of Soho – the center of new media, publishing, music and film in the UK's capital. It was a magnet for young graduates who could work in close proximity to their living quarters and the cafes, clubs and pubs that provided the locations for their leisure hours. It was a huge creative melting pot that, like all good warrens of talent, fed on itself.

Then some finance genius at Pearson had an idea. The real estate these people occupy is worth a lot of money. Let's sell it off and relocate our army of talent elsewhere. The bean counter was persuasive, and out went the people. But Pearson didn't move them around the corner. No, they moved them about 50 miles east of the capital to a greenfield site in Cambridgeshire, with a view of cows and sheep instead of London's iconic red double-decker buses. Well, in fact, they didn't really do that, because 70-plus percent of their talent voted with their feet and never made the move, taking redundancy instead. Now that is a lesson in how to turn off talent. This is especially dangerous when you do it in an industry where people are THE only asset you possess.

THE RISE OF THE LOBBYIST

No one quite knows when the lobbying profession really got serious. It has its beginnings in post-war America as an offshoot of Washington's Beltway law firms. Later it was also taken up by the major public relations firms. Today in the US it employs thousands of professionals all trying to jockey for position in putting the views and needs of their clients in front of the nation's lawmakers.

Lobbying exists everywhere there is a government and its satellite organizations making policy, so London, Berlin, Paris and Tokyo all have their cliques of lobby professionals. But nowhere has it taken off quite as big as in Brussels, home of the European Union. Current estimates say that there are at least 15,000 people involved in lobbying one way or another (and that could in fact be 25,000), making it a major employer in Europe's capital. And if you take into account the lobbyists outside of Brussels, Europe has something like 100,000 people engaged in this practice in one way or another.

Everyone is involved – needing to get their story heard – from industry trade associations to the major multinationals, from regional and city promoters to overseas lobby groups from countries who need to boost their trading credentials. They are all in town and in business.

For anyone seeking to break into the lobbying arena, there are several routes to get there. Many people arrive there through the legal profession, as there are an awful lot of lawyers involved, and some take the political route. However, the profession also has a large number of communications people. Indeed, one of the most interesting aspects of lobbying is that it requires a series of specialized skills coming together to make it work. So, face-to-face advocacy, communications and third-party endorsements are all part of the mix – and there are few (if any) people who can bring all these talents together.

There is also the question of who could teach all this stuff, so there is a dearth of formal programs to cover everything – you really do learn by experience. And, in looking to the workplace of tomorrow, lobbying probably offers one model of how that will develop in the future. As Richard Corliss, a director of Cambre Associates, a leading Brussels lobby firm, commented, "At the end of the day it comes down to individuals who have talents coming together to get a project achieved. As your career progresses, you might join up with a bigger group – or even work with several groups." He adds, "Then you might leave but keep your specialization going. Lobbying as a profession is constantly evolving. This really is all about hybrid employment models."

The second story is from New York, where some years ago the food company Campbell Soup had acquired the Belgian chocolate maker Godiva. Godiva had a great office in Manhattan. It needed that as the designers, marketers and media contact types who kept the brand alive not only wanted to work in the Big Apple, but they wanted to party there too. Again, a corporate bean counter stepped in. This time the trendily dressed, latte-sipping employees didn't face a trip to the country like their Pearson colleagues – they got sent to New Jersey instead. It's a long commute under the Hudson River to get to work in some inhospitable tower block, when you're young and creativity is running in your bloodstream. So, again, no one did it for very long.

Corporate bean counters need to learn from this. It is very costly to move people to a place they don't want to be. In fact it is a lot more costly than letting them do what they come to work for – to be productive, innovative and make money.

IT REALLY IS ABOUT YOU

You know that the unstoppable rise of social media has finally got somewhere truly significant when this happens: Britain's *Guardian* newspaper, one of the early adopters of the internet as an information place, has an annual award, the MediaGuardian "100," where they vote for the most influential people in the digital and media space. This year, ahead of Dick Costolo of Twitter and Larry Page of Google, they found a whole new number one. At number one they placed YOU. They qualified their choice by saying, "our panel wanted to use the No 1 spot to reflect the extent to which the individual had become empowered in the digital age." They continued, "Everyone can be a broadcaster-publisher in the digital era."

chapter 4
What the Workplace Looks Like

No one knows where the "ideal" workplace is. Talk to some stressed-out commuter on the 6:15 from Newhaven to New York and he'll tell you he wishes he was a telecommuter. Do the same with some work-at-home, creative dude in Southern California and he may be wishing for the camaraderie and problem-solving skills that are missing from his life. We humans are funny creatures; we never seem to be satisfied with where we live, or where we work.

And stories that the two, living and working, are coming together, so that the black of working and the white of leisure meld into some sort of grayscale lifestyle, aren't that clear either – in fact they are just that, GRAY.

What we are going to look at in this chapter is how the "workplace" is evolving. But we also speculate on the idea that it doesn't matter where you work, it is the work you do that counts. You may spend days with colleagues in an office-like space, but you may also need some downtime in order to concentrate on a major project. The one thing that makes this all come together is the ability to be linked up, to communicate with each other, face to face or at a distance – even a very great distance.

But let's start at the very beginning of the workplace – a long, long time ago.

OK, we'll skip the really early stuff and make the assumption that the smart kid who invented fire by bashing two flint rocks together kicked off something big. We'll fast forward a couple of millennia and get to ancient Rome. Civilization has arrived in the form of sanitation and hot water. Roman senators received their clients in the atriums of their villas – they were home workers. In medieval England, it was the court that was the model for the intelligentsia and the nobles. Most of the aristocracy were illiterate, so the monks had a busy time. They were the ecclesiastical hard drive, the memory card, of the system.

It was the Italians who changed things in a major way with the construction of the Uffizi Palace in Renaissance Florence. It was built in 1560 by the Medici family, as the offices for the Florentine magistrates – hence the name *"uffizi"* ("offices" in Italian). Architect and world-of-work expert, Andrew Chadwick,[1] explains that the spaces created are still recognizable today as offices; the forerunner of the cubbyholes of thousands of clerks and salary slaves of the next centuries. As Chadwick notes, "nothing much changes in the ensuing centuries – even the industrial revolution didn't change the basic model." And there it would all have stayed. We would still all be commuting to those big tower blocks if one thing had not happened – technology. New innovations, especially the arrival of the digital world, meant that we didn't have to work in the same place every day. We were finally free of the shackles of being in one place at one time.

While we can't yet bend time to suit our needs, we can partake in collaborative work from around the other side of the globe – assuming we get the time right. One of the reasons – seldom thought about – as to why London is such a successful city is that during its work day it can interact with both the Americas and Asia on easy time cycles. When it's 8 a.m. in London, it's 3 p.m. in Hong Kong; when it's 4 p.m. in London, it's 11 a.m. in New York and 8 a.m. in Los Angeles. Throw in the ease – and cost-effectiveness – of services such as Skype, Go-to-Meeting and

---

[1] Andrew Chadwick is the founder and principal of Chadwick International, an award-winning architectural firm headquartered in London, and is a partner of the FutureWork Forum.

Cisco's Telepresence and you can have high-quality multi-location conferences at the click of a mouse.

It's what you do

Certainly the most important thing that I have learned from the research for this book is that "where" you are is irrelevant and it is "what" you do that is the key element. As IBM researcher Susan Stucky pointed out earlier in the book, it is the ability to link digitally (whether around the world or down the corridor) that defines how projects are created and completed.

This is important, because every week in the media we are bombarded with the results of surveys and the musings of experts about whether working from home, working remotely or working in an office with hundreds or thousands of others is the best way. The answer to all these "chatterings and tweetings" of what's good or bad is – "it doesn't matter. You're missing the point entirely!" Work gets done in the best way possible by the best people to do it. That's called being efficient. Jobs are not split into just two categories of those who work from home and those who don't. Most job-holders operate on a mixed working experience, spending two or three days with their colleagues and other days at home or (and this is the other big group) working on-site at client locations.

A study by the cutely named Uci2i, a UK video conference firm, of 1,000 workers, found that home-based workers spend almost an extra month each year working than their office-based colleagues. This is not recognized at all by the office workers, who, according to the study, think home workers are "cheating the system." Ninety-four percent of the home workers and office workers polled said that home workers produce better work. The reasons given were less commuting stress and a consequent improvement on work–life balance.

Virtual walls

Another study of 2,000 workers in the US for the design company Gensler reported that office workers were being disturbed by the trend toward open-plan workspaces. According to the survey, nine out of ten people polled said that duties that needed deep concentration (such as programming and reading or writing complex material) were critical of their job environment. With email and other digital links replacing the phone or face-to-face chat, even socialization and collaboration tasks had become solitary, screen-based activities. The report said that "many workers now simply choose to put on headphones to cut out the external world, creating virtual walls between colleagues."

The problem with these kinds of surveys and well-meaning advice is that they just scratch the surface of the workplace issue. They try – and fail – to pigeonhole world-of-work issues with old-fashioned notions of what jobs are. They want to divide us into people who work in an "office" environment and those who work from home. It just isn't like that.

Indeed, my own research amongst work colleagues and friends has produced the following results:

Friends and work colleagues who work *full time* for an organization:

- Work at main office location   30%
- Work at client locations   30%
- Work at home   30%
- Work while traveling (hotel etc.) 10%

Friends and work colleagues who work *freelance*

- Work at home office or shared office   40%
- Work at client location   20%
- Work at client's customer location   30%
- Work while traveling (hotel etc.)   10%

Now that's more like it! This is the reality of work today. And if you take those numbers above you can probably apply them anywhere around the world – at least anywhere with a modern, linked-up infrastructure that supports a highly trained working population. So that's what our business leaders, government leaders, trend-spotters and the rest need to take on board. Work today – jobs today – are a patchwork quilt of activity. And over days, months, years the mix of time spent in one place will change dramatically.

Indeed, as Jim Ware,[2] a San Francisco-based workplace consultant stresses, "If I am right, in just a few years there may be a 'typical' workday for you, and one for me. But they won't be the same. And, my workday today will be different from yesterday and different still from tomorrow." He adds, "I'll work differently from moment to moment, depending on the task I'm engaged in, the other people I am collaborating with and the place where I happen to be."

And he is hugely enthusiastic about the future: "Just look at the tremendous variety in workplaces and work-related technologies that are in use today. To the extent that we will be able to configure our work environments to fit our individual needs, we'll be more productive, more engaged and more satisfied."

Jim Ware is a true believer that things are changing (and already have to a large extent) and that it is the ability to collaborate instantly in this digital age that defines work and jobs too: "Just about everyone I know, from software programmers to customer service representatives, collaborates every day with people who are somewhere else. Sometimes our collaborators are customers, sometimes colleagues, sometimes vendors or consultants – and sometimes they are completely unknown individuals whose ideas we come across (and comment on) in an article or a tweet."

That reference to social media takes us back to the comments of researcher Susan Stucky in Chapter 1 where she emphasized that it is the digital presence that allows us to complete tasks in hitherto unimagined ways.

---

[2] Jim Ware is the founder and managing partner of The Future of Work ... unlimited and a partner of the FutureWork Forum.

Two pioneers of remote working, Kate Lister and Tom Harnish,[3] are fairly certain that we are only at the beginning of what's possible. "That digital world is going to be everywhere," they say, "no blind spots." Indeed, they forecast that very soon, "We think people will expect high speed (50mps or better) internet access everywhere – like electricity and water. When governments understand that the value of information highways is as great as concrete and asphalt highways, it will transform what we call 'work' faster than anything else."

Once that global web is complete and there are no dark corners that cannot be reached, then we have the ability to work and collaborate with anyone we choose – interacting closely with people who live a world away and whom we may never (most probably won't) physically meet. And that collaboration can and will produce results as yet unimagined.

As Jim Ware says, "Exchanging tweets and blog comments may not seem like real-time collaboration, but they do produce the experience of an ongoing, active conversation characterized by learning, teaching and co-creation – the very essence of real collaboration."

The collective hive mind

Jim Ware continues, "There is a growing number of anecdotes and case examples of companies using the power of social media to tap into the collective 'hive mind' of thousands of people all over the world." Ware cites the example of Procter & Gamble, the consumer products firm that is "using the power of crowd-sourcing to pull research scientists into global conversations about new products and get feedback from customers." And he adds, "many other global companies are now using high-definition video conferencing to enable distributed meetings every day. There are now thousands of collaborative whiteboards and distributed brainstorming technologies in use for all kinds of virtual communities."

---

[3] Kate Lister is President of Global Workplace Analytics. Tom Harnish is Senior Scientist and President of the Telework Research Network.

Tom Harnish and Kate Lister agree and add: "In a lot of what is ready to happen, bandwidth is the pivotal constraint. But when that's fixed, it's not hard to imagine a 'window' on the wall that will let you see outside in high definition from a home office in the basement. You'll also be able to see others as a group or individually as if they were in the room, run by something like a Siri/Google voice command, 'OK Wall, let me see Mike.'"

And Harnish and Lister add that chief executives and government heads are going to have to really think about a lot of this development in new ways because it will transform how we communicate and collaborate with each other. They envisage "long promised, but never delivered, usable and affordable teleconferencing from cameras everywhere. Wall-size displays will transform the meaning of connected." And they expect that "sight, not sound" will eventually become the new currency of work. They make a point that we should all heed: "Not long ago, a telephone number was a place (on a desk, wall or phone booth). Today a number is a person. The same, we think, will happen with work. Overused, but still true nonetheless, work is something you DO – not a place you GO."

It can be more than that. Architect Andrew Chadwick has long been advocating that the next big thing in communication technology will be the use of holograms (scientifically possible, right now). He believes that in the not too distant future we will be able to create 3D holograms in the images of ourselves and "transport" ourselves to meetings, without any need to fly or suffer jet lag. "You can program a hologram with a series of commands or to say 'yes' or 'no' depending on the question," he enthuses. We may never be able to teleport ourselves, but we may well be able to do the next best thing with a clone-like facsimile.

The rise of the distributed team

Most work, as many of the people featured in this book have said, is based on projects. And projects tend to be run by teams. Today, when we require a vast array of skills to complete a task, many of those teams are spread around the city, the country, the world.

Remote teams, distributed teams, whatever you call them, have been a feature of the workplace for a long, long time. But, just as the office-bound worker thinks his home-working colleague is goofing off for most of the day, so there are still managers and supervisors who have great difficulty in managing, never mind motivating, people they can't see. While much of the technology breakthroughs that Chadwick, Ware, Harnish and Lister predict should make it certain that you can at least see the remote worker, you'll have to consider the idea that – as with all human endeavors – once someone has developed something, there is another human who will come along and mess with it (see box below).

There are a lot of predictions floating around in this chapter, so I thought it was time to add my own. This is not designed purely as a little light relief from the seriousness of the future workplace. It is a warning from the future. For anyone who has worked with real humans and not just the bits and bytes of the digital space, there are a few points that may well strike a chord and are worth keeping in mind. Technology changes – humans don't. Well not that much anyway!

THE FUTURE OF WORK? ... WELL, IT'S REAL LIFE IN A VIRTUAL HAYSTACK

Today, most employees spend upwards of 15 percent of their workday digitally "goofing off," surfing the net, selling online or seeking out great travel deals (this practically doubles for "dispersed" or at-home workers). That 15 percent accounts for the supposed increase in productivity over the last decade that technology has "won" for us.

Think carefully now. Isn't it all SO predictable? Work in the future will be the same as work today, as work was yesterday. Mr and Ms Average will try very, very hard to do as little of it as possible. Oh sure, there'll be the super-rich CEOs and their hangers-on, but the rest of us will be doing the mid-21st-century equivalent of the 19th-century farm worker dozing in a haystack on a summer's afternoon.

By 2050 emergent digital technology will enable the worker of tomorrow to goof off in the real world, virtual world or whatever other worlds we come up with. Playing hooky from work will never have had so many possibilities and opportunities – or been so easy.

Don't believe those Big Brother – "they are watching your every move" – predictions. Those with technology smarts will use them not for the good of the mega corporation but so that they (and all the people they know) can goof off as much as they like. The guys and gals who work with this stuff are the 21st-century equivalent of plumbers. These people KNOW how to make it work for THEM: always did, always will. Dickens' Artful Dodger has a permanent place in the world of tomorrow, only it isn't pockets he picks – have you seen what a ten-year-old with a laptop can already do today?

So in 2050, what have we got? Technology is ubiquitous and the more you have the more you need protection from the virtual pickpocket. But overall, employees and outworkers are freer. Indeed, the packages you can buy assure you of the opposite of Big Brother interference – they assure you total anonymity. And this is backed up by tough global laws on data-mining and intrusive spying on those who work for you. Companies today may want to spend some time thinking about this.

What about those left out of the ongoing technology developments? Well, I'm not sure there will be any. In the digital world of 2050, when an electronic chip – or whatever it is by then – is cheaper than a potato chip, it is more likely to be open access for all (but that's another story for next time).

In 2050 we can do what WE want – the same as we could in 1850. It was only the late 20th and early 21st centuries that got us going in the wrong direction.

> Hooray for the future of work! It's going to be a lot more like it used to be – even if you are going to have to goof off in a virtual haystack, rather than a real one. Never mind, the smell of freedom will still be as sweet!

Managing remote teams, even with all the technology available, is hard. While some will say that it is all about common sense and keeping things as simple and open as possible, there are a few things that anyone trying to run a team at a distance, be it in the next town or on the other side of the world, needs to keep in mind. Here are a few thoughts:

- Leaders of dispersed teams need to keep top of mind that communication skills are critically important to the team's effectiveness. The opportunities for misunderstanding (communicating in different languages and understanding other cultures) are far greater on a dispersed team.
- Problems can be increased – even with video links – by a lack of face-to-face contact and a corresponding reduction in non-verbal signs (body language is a major information conduit between people).
- Contact by email and phones can miss out a lot of finer points that a face-to-face group don't have to put up with.
- Dispersed teams often face difficulties sharing information inside the group as a consequence of taking longer to build up trust in each other.
- Project management, in particular, can be a problem as the team struggles to schedule dates and times for meetings.

Kate Lister and Tom Harnish put another item on their distributed teams' list: "A new role for managers who have remote workers is acting as advocate and mentor," they say. "People are spread around the globe and virtually invisible (or is it invisibly virtual!). Unless managers tout the achievements of their subordinates, career progression will be more difficult."

And building effective at-a-distant teams also means that for many a manager and supervisor they will have to respect that work cycles are not going to follow traditional nine to five patterns. Here's Jim Ware's view on that: "We are certainly going to see much more variety in work cycles," he says. "Many companies are currently experimenting with '9x80,' bi-weekly cycles, in which people still put in 80 hours over two weeks but they do it in nine days rather than ten. I've also experienced some instances of '4x40,' meaning 40 hours over four days, rather than five."

Ware continues: "And, of course, we have all heard about the Silicon Valley tech companies that let employees set their own hours – as long as they are available for team meetings. There are certainly people who prefer to work (and work more productively) in the wee hours of the morning, then sleep until noon. If their work patterns don't involve others, or affect the schedule, what difference does it make?"

He makes one final, important, point: "If we only learn to measure and reward work 'outcomes,' rather than work 'activity,' this kind of individual diversity becomes far easier to imagine and coordinate."

Indeed, this is the greatest advantage of all from the digital age. Far from lumping us all together into a nightmare 1984 Orwellian scenario where we are little better than numbers, the digital revolution allows each of us to own our own identity, even if it is prefaced with a cell phone number and an email address.

Offices won't disappear

With technology assuming an ever greater role in the workplace, what future is there for the office? More than that, what's next for the corporate headquarters, once the symbol of an organization's health and vitality? Well, in talking to a great many people, it seems that the office block is not only alive but being used just as much as ever.

Head to Silicon Valley, supposedly the fountainhead of all that's cool and new, and you'll see that today's corporate success stories – the likes of Google, Facebook and Apple – are not building offices, they're creating whole new campuses. They may be, in their fixtures and fittings, a long way from the office block of old with its warrens of cubicles and corner offices to aspire to, but it is still a lot of people in one specific place for one stated purpose. Indeed, in Silicon Valley, Facebook has just moved into a refurbished set of offices originally built by Sun Microsystems (then purchased by Oracle). Not to be outdone, Korean electronics giant, Samsung, is building a massive new research lab. Of course the talking point of the Valley was when the CEO of Yahoo!, Marissa Mayer, banned her employees from working from home. In the freewheeling culture of Silicon Valley geek-land this was the ultimate in non-cool decision-making.

But as locally based Jim Ware – who is certainly well placed to watch the action – says: "Over time, I believe we will see less of a corporate footprint, as more and more companies seek to save money with less real estate and institute desk-sharing programs and smaller workstations, plus a much higher percentage of collaborative space ... Most of us – including me – still believe that in-person meetings are the most effective vehicle for creative idea generation – although I am sure we are going to see the development of increasingly powerful technologies that will make remote collaboration almost as effective as actually being there." Let's hear a round of applause for Andrew Chadwick's holograms!

Across the Atlantic, Google has announced plans to spend £650 million on a new London HQ of 725,000 square feet that will accommodate 4,500 staff – its first purpose-built offices anywhere in the world. The new HQ will rise up in the King's Cross area of the city, which is becoming a new growth district, in part because of its excellent transport links for commuters and its proximity to St Pancras International for trains to Brussels, Paris and beyond. More major corporations are moving into the area, including the publisher of this book; Macmillan is consolidating all their UK staff in just-completed offices.

Head east down the River Thames and you come to Canary Wharf – home of the world's bankers and financiers. There, in an area rundown for years, has been created a totally new city. Amazingly, people live and work and play there without any need to leave the area. It's modern, clean, relatively crime free and home to some of the toniest restaurants, clubs and bars anywhere. In fact it's just a modern-day version of that greatest of places to work, live and play – Manhattan.

It would seem that as long as we humans want to huddle together – that hive instinct – we'll go on inhabiting collective places that are both areas in which to collaborate and statements of what our business stands for and the culture it represents.

Hubs for early adopters

That people need to congregate together has no finer example than the increase in popularity of innovation hubs and the like, office locations where start-ups can find a home with like-minded people. These may have had their birth in the geek-land of Silicon Valley back in the 1990s, but they are fast becoming established as a favorite way to do business. They have a terrific set of advantages over other forms of office space:

- They are available by the day, week or month at affordable rates.
- Many have multiple locations (nationwide or even globally).
- They offer workspace and meeting space as you need it.
- They provide back-office services if you need them.
- They are "cool" places to work – or even just to hang out and soak up the creative vibe.
- They allow people to mix with others – great ways for promoting your business, getting new clients and getting problems solved.

Some hubs even offer a lot more. The Innovation Birmingham Campus, at the Aston Science Park in the UK's Midlands, houses around 50 start-ups. While the building is nothing spectacular, a typical glass office block from the 1960s, the interior is a buzz of activity. This is the home of the Birmingham end of the EU-funded "Entrepreneurs for the Future" incubation program. To qualify you need to be an innovative tech start-up that is capable of launching into a revenue- and profit-generating company.

The Aston Science Park is a serious operation. Start-ups that qualify get a lot – and it's free. Well, it's free for six months to get you going. The Entrepreneurs for the Future program gives would-be business creators a package worth £10,000:

- Mentoring, personalized to your business objectives.
- Free access and invites to more than 80 business and industry events to get your product or service out there.
- Desk space (totally rent free) with phone service and mailbox.
- 24/7 access to the offices and all their back-up facilities, allowing you to work to a schedule that suits you.
- Access to special drop-in sessions on-site, such as seminars and advice on finance, PR, marketing and HR issues.
- 2Fbit/s broadband.
- Access to dedicated meeting room facilities.

From humble beginnings at the Science Park, companies have gone on to create viable organizations in the high-tech space. More than that, they have created jobs for a growing number of people who would otherwise be filling the unemployment queue.

Peer-to-peer

The Science Park's head of communications Charlotte Crossley says that what makes a good entrepreneur, those most likely to succeed, is people with such key traits as "the ability to sell a concept or product, be an all-round marketer and able to get the trust of would-be investors." She adds that "the greatest thing about the Science Park is the peer-to-peer aspect. There are countless examples here of start-ups that you may expect would be competing for the same business. But they actually proactively work together and become the best of friends."

On the flip side, what about the bad news: why do many start-ups sink without trace? According to Crossley, "Lack of match-funding is the biggest issue. There is so often an offer on the table from a funding organization, but there's typically a requirement that it needs to be match-funded by private angel investors. That's a challenge to meet in the current economic climate."

In other locations around the globe, innovation hubs have been popping up like mushrooms in a field in autumn. All of them have the same overall theme running through them – providing a creative, collaborative space and connectivity at an affordable price.

Some people use them as a permanent place to hang their hat, others use them as a place to get away from the home-working atmosphere and add a dash of professional inclusion to their lives. One hub operation in the US actually has on its menu of rooms and creative pods to rent a choice for a "Cone of Silence" – an insulated room, precisely what some people need in order to think through their latest idea.

Hubs are sometimes more than just a commercially minded operation. Ryan Coonerty and Jeremy Neuner, creators of NextSpace, say that their aim was to combine business and social in one. They describe NextSpace as a place where "we provide innovative physical and virtual infrastructure that freelancers, entrepreneurs and creative class professionals need to succeed in the 21st-century knowledge economy." They go on to explain that, "in an increasingly disconnected world, NextSpace creates a collaborative community that is revolutionizing the nature of work."

All this makes sense, except that the phrase "increasingly disconnected world" doesn't ring true at all. We are connected more than ever, but we can do that without seeing each other, if that's what works.

In addition to building NextSpace, Coonerty and Neuner are authors of the book *The Rise of the Naked Economy – How to Benefit from the Changing Workplace*,[4] which reports on how, "from corner coffee shops

---

[4] Palgrave Macmillan, 2013.

to Fortune 500 companies, workers from all different backgrounds are creating a new reality and prosperity."

NextSpace is only one of many of these operations around the globe. The HUB is a network of innovative spaces that are set to circle the world. Founded in London in 2005 (there are now four of them in that city), another 30 are open, with over 50 more in the planning stage, spread across five continents. Their tagline on promotion materials sums up the operation: "the HUB is about the power of innovation through collaboration."

With a similar goal to NextSpace, the company says in its online brochure that they "set out to create spaces that combine the best of a trusted community, innovation lab, business incubator and the comforts of home." They add that these are "Spaces with all the tools and trimmings needed to grow and develop innovative ventures for the world. But, above all, spaces for meaningful encounters, exchange and inspiration, full of diverse people doing amazing things." Just by the tone of the copywriter (who no doubt works at the HUB) you can tell that this is London, England.

NextSpace is a little more laid-back Californian in its promotion. "NextSpace gives our members a reason to get out of their jammies in the morning," it declares brightly.

And NextSpace's founders haven't finished yet – they are still innovating. The latest product is NextKids, a workspace for parents and a care space for children, where "both parent and child can thrive, equally, without compromise – in the same location." They add in their promotional blurb, "We invite you to experience a new way of living, working and caring for your children the way we were always meant to – together."

Could NextPets be just a step away, we would have to ask?

It's indie auction time

It is the rise of the innovation hub that has eventually led to something else entirely – the use of the basic tenets of crowd-sourcing to create a whole new way of offering creative services. Already there are a lot of these organizations out there (crowdSPRING, Odesk, Elance, Fiverr and 99 Designs amongst them). The idea is simple. You, or your organization, want a new design, a translation, a piece of copy written. You tell the service what you want and they put it out to their online members. Members submit ideas and you choose what you want and pay an agreed price for it. The only problem is that it has really pushed down prices to ridiculous levels as everyone tries to undercut each other.

Reports from some US cities suggest that these services have destroyed carefully nurtured teams of designers, who simply can't make any money since this phenomenon started. Amateurs and people trying to break into the creative business are doing things for practically free.

So there is another – perhaps much darker – side to all this technology. While it frees us to collaborate in totally new ways, it also makes some things economically untenable. No doubt there will eventually be a course correction and something will snap in the system. However, it shows how new technologies have a habit of not just changing how we do things, but destroying things that already work well.

The human need for strongpoints

All this reliance on digital technology and the virtual world, as well as drop-in centers and non-permanent places to work, has architect Andrew Chadwick worried. "The predictions seem to have all come true," he suggests, "technology has liberated real estate from its shackles, people can, and do, work everywhere, anytime – you no longer need an office. But," he continues, "we humans haven't really caught up yet, have we? Our ingrained habits and feelings make us ever so slightly uncomfortable with this 24/7 peripatetic world. What we need as humans are strongpoints, places where we can behave defensively, where we can retreat away from this world we have created. And," he warns, "the more technology advances, the more we will need them."

He has a good point here and one that is worth some lengthy consideration. The military define a strongpoint as "a location that is by its site and nature easily defended." Maybe that is what all of us need. After a hard day at the innovation hub, or collaborating with our work colleagues around the globe, won't we need a space that is ours and ours alone? I believe we used to call it "home," but that won't work too well if most of us spend at least half our time working from our homes – that former place of sanctuary from the big world outside.

> **DO NOT DISTURB**
> If we, as humans, need strongpoints in our lives, then they have to be very, very personal. A great example is provided by the writer and children's author Roald Dahl. Deep in his garden at home was his "writing house," a place only he was allowed to enter. No one was allowed to interrupt him once he was ensconced inside – even if it was on fire!

In fact Chadwick's idea that everyone needs a strongpoint – a place of retreat – in their lives, runs counter to some of his other ideas. A few years ago his firm, Chadwick International, won an architectural prize with a concept that he termed "the Elastic Environment."[5] In this environment, the worlds of work and play not only came together, but morphed from one to the other (there's a video link in the footnote). This elastic environment meant that you could occupy a single space for all your needs, but the physical space would change as required. One minute a breakfast bar, the next an office, then a meeting room, a gym and so on.

Chadwick is certain this will be the face of the home and office in 50 years' time, with sentient materials, modelled on 3D printers, making it all possible. The only thing he, and us, need to work out is where we will place our personal strongpoint in this future space.

A model for the future?

Possibly the last place you would expect to find any kind of workplace innovation is in the corridors of a government ministry. The phrase

---

[5] "The Elastic Environment," Chadwick International. See www.chadwick-international.com.

"government ministry" conjures up instant images of bored, clock-watching clerks, corridors full of files and a lot of desks – rows of them, all the same. And, indeed, that's just what Belgium's Ministry of Social Security looked like a few years ago. Housed in an office tower block in the center of Brussels, the Ministry was like thousands of others around the world – an uninspiring and unloved place to work.

That was before the current Director of Social Security Services in Belgium took over. What Frank Van Massenhove proposed was nothing short of a revolution. Take all the files and turn them into e-records, make it possible for everyone – if they wish – to work from home.

Van Massenhove and his team sold the idea to the government and went to work on the plan. One of the biggest hurdles was getting the buy-in from Belgium's powerful – and resistant to change – trade unions. But that worked too.

Now – some two years into the program – there is no paper in the offices. Anything left on a desk gets shredded by the cleaning crew. Van Massenhove said that after a "few incidents" at the beginning, everyone learned very quickly!

Huge numbers of staff work at home. Not all the time, but as and when they feel like it – or if they have child care issues. I visited on a snowy day in January. Naively, I asked Van Massenhove if all the staff were stranded by the snowstorm? He laughed, "Of course not, they are all working at home, because they don't need to come into work."

One of the keys to the Ministry's success was the ability of the technology professionals to be able to create security firewalls for all the staff (they are working on files for pensions and sickness benefits and so on). And now they have gone further than that. In the last phase they have been able to let their staff choose what computers and other technology they want to work with. This ability to use anything that suits makes the whole operation even more user-friendly.

Not only have they saved desk space – no one has an assigned desk, you sit where you like and take your "file" with you – but they have saved the cost of an additional building in the center of the city that just held the paper files. The whole office is light and airy; open plan meeting rooms and colorful chairs and wall hangings make it look more like a design studio than a government establishment.

So successful has this man from the ministry been that private sector clients are now consulting him and his team on how to do the same. Furthermore, they have won a series of prestigious prizes, including Company of the Year and HR Manager of the Year awards.

What the Belgian Ministry example goes to show is that good workplaces that please the people can be created anywhere. All it takes is some vision and a real enthusiasm and commitment. The staff at Belgium's Ministry of Social Security were lucky that they had a man with real vision in charge. In addition, they were very, very lucky that he was able to do the most important thing – sell the idea to his political masters and then enthuse everyone to get behind the project.

In the US, another fusty, traditional organization has been given a makeover too. Lawyers at the US Patent and Trademark Office (PTO) don't have coveted single offices or cubicles anymore. They review all those patent applications from home. The work they do doesn't require them to be on-site and doesn't require them to meet with clients. Today, two-thirds of the staff of 11,000 telework – 4,000 of them do it five days a week.

The result of this radical move is that the average home-working PTO employee spends 66.3 hours more each year (yes, it is a government department after all and they measure these things) examining applications than their office-based colleagues. That works out (now we are getting really picky!) to about 3.5 reviews. The good part is that the backlog of patent applications (about 600,000 at the time of writing) is going down and the agency saves $17 million a year in office space and related costs.

So why aren't more of us thinking along these lines? Is it just back to the point of "what we don't see, we can't measure"? If so, we need to do something radical about the managers and supervisors we employ, not the technology we use.

India without aircon

Radically different workplace solutions can be anywhere – as the Belgian Ministry and the US Patent Office examples have shown. What they all have in common is a refusal to follow the herd and a desire to drastically rethink how people should work or how the infrastructure they use should be created.

Bangalore is Southern India's answer to Silicon Valley, and with a population of eight million it is India's third largest city. But severe infrastructure strains have made energy efficiency a very real necessity. Shimoga, 150 miles north of Bangalore, is the site of a newly built office complex for the outsourcing company Xchanging. Designed by London-based Chadwick International with Buro Happold, an engineering firm that specializes in low energy-use projects, the idea was to do something different in the construction of the building. The usual thing in the area is "to build a glass box and stuff it full of aircon," says Dan Knott, Buro Happold's project chief. He adds, "what's remarkable about this project in Shimoga is that it has no air conditioning in a climate where the average temperatures are 34–36°C. The climate is not at all hospitable and an unsealed building that harks back to old-fashioned traditions is nothing short of revolutionary – above all, of course, it's cheap! And with no aircon there are no complex building management technologies to go wrong."

"India is all about cheap," says project architect Andrew Chadwick, wryly. He was the man who challenged Buro Happold to create a building in one of the hottest places on the planet with no aircon at all. Aircon, in this kind of climate, makes up around 40 percent of the running costs of a building. Using careful siting of the building to shade critical areas from the sun, and four huge wind scoops that form the roof, the designers have been able to create a workplace for 1,000 people with no aircon and that reduces temperature by as much as 5°C.

According to Buro Happold's calculations, the savings from constructing another 1,300 Shimoga-style buildings in place of those traditional glass boxes would equal the output of a 1GW power station. Such environmental savings cannot be ignored on a warming planet.

Best companies, doing best things

However, there is more than just technology and new-style workspaces. You can build all sorts of workplace structures but, as I keep stressing, the human aspect is also key. So, are there any new developments in how we work, apart from allowing for greater flexibility in when and where – are organizations trying out anything new?

Well, looking around the globe, apart from a lot more concentration on the corporate culture, the answer would have to be "No." We really haven't invented that much. Let's look at what the so-called "25 Best Places to Work Around the World" are doing and why they got voted in. Amazingly, of the 25 companies, 20 are in the US, which doesn't seem to be quite right. Employees vote for their own firm, so it may be something to do with stuffing the virtual ballot box. Anyway, here are some possible learning points from them, but be warned: there's absolutely nothing radical here; nothing exciting at all.

1st   SAS Institute: The exciting point is that the CEO hosts what are termed "Conversations Over Coffee," and are billed as "informal, no pressure gatherings."

2nd   Google: Employees report that "there are plenty of places in Silicon Valley where you can make money fast, but Google is a place you can call home." It seems that Google employees have found their strongpoint.

3rd   NetApp: They have cultural and business sessions, with the unfortunate acronym of TOAST. This stands for Training on all Special Things.

4th   Kimberly-Clark: Before starting their job, new hires receive a welcome package in the mail that contains information about the job and company, an email from their "Godfather"

	(mentor) and a key – "symbolic of opening the door of the best company."
5th	Microsoft: Since 2000, the company has operated Digigirlz (yes, that's the correct spelling) to encourage more women to pursue careers in technology. The program hosts events for girls in high school.
6th	Marriott: The managers host life-skills sessions for employees (it has 325,000 employees around the globe), teaching things such as how to open a bank account and how to get a loan.
7th	Federal Express: The company has a policy to recruit older employees into the workforce and a strong culture of volunteerism linked to its connections with international aid agencies.
8th	W. L. Gore: Every employee (called associates) has a mentor to help them succeed on their chosen career path.
9th	Diageo: Lots of employee participation in good causes.
10th	Autodesk: Great sabbatical program – six weeks of paid time off every four years on top of usual vacation and holidays.
11th	PepsiCo: Appears to be a generally good all-round place to work.
12th	Ernst & Young: Involve junior staffers in leadership opportunities. The company sends more than 2,300 interns from 27 countries to its International Intern Leadership Conference.
13th	Telefonica: Spain's top telecomms firm has a Global Rotation Program that allows employees to spend six months working on a specific project at a Telefonica office in another country.
14th	Monsanto: Great at recognizing emerging talent within the organization.
15th	Intel: New hires at Intel have dedicated greeters and gifts waiting for them when they arrive.
16th	National Instruments: The inventors of "sneaker management." This is not spying on employees, but senior executives (including the CEO) "walking around and visiting with the employees."
17th	General Mills: "Connect is General Mills' internal global networking site, available to all employees." The company

explains that: "It fosters connectedness and the exchange of ideas and interests among co-workers."

18th American Express: "A group of four or five leaders get together and surprise their co-workers with flowers or a gift *in front of their colleagues* [my italics] to celebrate their accomplishments."

19th Accor: This French hospitality giant has an active program that allows employees to switch countries as they progress in their careers.

20th McDonald's: They've now got seven Hamburger Universities, where workers learn at "the hands of full-time restaurant operation professors."

21st Cisco: Big on connectivity.

22nd Novo Nordisk: A Danish healthcare firm that emphasizes three responsibilities: social, financial and environmental.

23rd Quintiles: A highly successful employee referral program. One-fifth of new hires are recommended by existing employees.

24th S. C. Johnson: Every office has its own "Now Thanks!" program which provides "on-the-spot recognition for great work with praise and a monetary reward."

25th Mars: Big on training and development – "available in 22 languages."

Well, I don't know about you, but I find these worldwide winners to be a pretty staid bunch. Not much excitement or even originality to be found amongst them. True, you could argue that these are big corporations with thousands of employees, but although certain standards need to apply on a global scale, surely the biggest thing you can do is treat people as individuals.

Now when you look at smaller companies (those places where innovation really is breaking out like a rash), things get a lot more interesting.

The 2012 Best Small Workplace in the US award went to Oregon-based Ruby Receptionists. Ultra-friendly receptionists are the hallmark of this virtual receptionist firm. Three of the full-time employees are dedicated solely to ensuring a strong culture: Director of Culture, Office Champion and the Rubynator. Quarterly games and competitions reward employees for creating what is described as "meaningful connections in an increasingly virtual, technology-focused world."

Another winner, Radio Flyer, manufactures those iconic little red wagons that kids pull around. The company is "pulled along by its Chief Wagon Officer," who takes every opportunity to communicate the "Little Red Rule." Employees are referred to as, what else – "Flyers!"

Dixon Schwabl, an advertising and marketing agency in New York, has an in-house band, called Afternoon Socks, tied in to a tradition of people changing their socks on long workdays.

Where are the innovators?

I must admit I'm a bit disappointed in the pride of the world's (OK, then, America's) corporations when it comes to getting employees to embrace their workplace. But it seems, to this writer and researcher at least, that we aren't nearly as creative as we used to be 10 and 20 years ago. Either that or all the uber-cool people have left the big corporations (there's some anecdotal evidence they are doing so anyway) and are plugged in at their local innovation hub.

Looking back over a couple of decades of discovering the wild and the whacky things that get employees fired up I seem to recall the following, and they were much more innovative than today:

- When Ben & Jerry still owned Ben & Jerry's ice cream (it was sold to food conglomerate Unilever in 2000) they used to do fun things like having a "come to work as Elvis day."
- Those nice people from Novo Nordisk are doing good things, but there's a wonderful, small pharmaceutical company in Denmark that has a "company dog." Employees needing a break or quiet time just take the dog from the front reception and go for a walk.
- Back in the last century – the 20th that is – I had a great friend who ran a Madison Avenue advertising agency. This was just as

computers – and the VDU screen - took hold. My friend modified a golf cart to look like a pizza truck and drove down the corridors (it fitted into the elevator) ringing the bell and offering free slices of pizza. His goal, "To get people talking to each other again."
- In California – the fountainhead of whacky employee ploys – there were "Bring Your Pet to Work Days." Someone brought their pet python, which ate someone's cat.
- Then there were the organizations where people worked late and could dial down for a gourmet meal to take home.
- Others offered a supermarket delivery service, a dry cleaning and laundry service and a drop-off Amazon and eBay service and the same for returns.

Maybe it's time we all got a little more creative. Having said that, here are some things we might want to learn, and perhaps even adopt, from some "Best People Practices" of 2012.

- Walks and talks: Fit CEOs and senior managers, who want the same for their employees, are taking them out for a run or a fast walk, instead of that cup of coffee in the canteen.
- Some companies are giving their new employees a notebook (the coolest are either loaning them or even giving them a tablet) to record interesting things they learn about the company in the early days. After a set period there's a discussion about how any of this could improve the job or their workplace.
- "Hack Days:" These are full-day sessions where employees come together and spend time developing an idea that makes the product, company or office better.

What we get out of all this is the simple fact that some people fit in with a culture, others don't. There are places listed above that a lot of people would find a nightmare to work in, whereas others would embrace them in a heartbeat. One of the keys to being successful and being a useful, productive employee is knowing the type of business and then, equally important, the culture of the company you want to be in. What you need to know is that when someone says, "that's just the way we do business around here," you agree with it. That's exactly what Chapter 5 is all about.

Home-working isn't new

We began this chapter with a short history lesson about the workplace. Let's end that way too, and show that home-working isn't some modern-day idea.

In 1761 the solicitor of the Scottish Board of Customs in Edinburgh reported his difficulties in getting to the office (it is not recorded why), and asked if he could work from home. The Board agreed to his request and granted him an allocation of five pounds (weight) of candles.

Even then, there were enlightened employers who saw that work was not about place, but the quantity and quality of what you did.

chapter 5
Making a Career Inside or Outside the Organization

As we've established in previous chapters, there are many opportunities in the world of work, and individuals have a huge choice in the way they can pursue a career. But whether you choose to work for a major corporation, a SME or become an entrepreneur, there are a lot of issues to overcome if you are going to succeed.

In some ways, it would appear that none of us are getting this right. Recruiters complain that people looking for a job are either ill-qualified or don't have the right attitude. Those searching say that companies don't understand their needs and don't treat them as individuals. People looking to start up their own business say that they can't get funds and can't get access to begin to sell their ideas.

The disconnect between recruiter and job seeker today is wide indeed, but whatever the frustrations on both sides, these are the realities of the workplace of today.

The Generation Europe Foundation (GEF) is a Brussels-based think tank and research group that looks at a whole range of issues, especially for those just starting out in their careers. Their view is that too many first-time job seekers make the major mistake of not really working out what they want to do with their professional lives. GEF's Managing Director, Christina Fancello, says that "you need to figure out early on what you enjoy doing and what you want to get out of a job. Once you really know what your goals are, it's easier to define a career path and stick with a plan."

Fancello adds that "it's not all about academic results. When you ask yourself, 'what do I do well?', the answer doesn't have to be 'maths, sciences or languages.' You might say, 'I have a huge network of friends,' or 'I organize great parties.' They too are skills. So look at what you're good at and try and find equivalents in the working world."

The key to this is to be very honest with yourself. The best way to do that is to get a friend, or a group of friends, to go through the process with you and be honest about your ambitions. It is also a question of what suits one person might be a nightmare job scenario for another. For example, you can use this analogy to get the idea of what you need to consider:

Question: What do chefs and airline pilots have in common? Answer: they both work in mostly cramped conditions, under a lot of pressure for long hours. Therefore, no matter how good your piloting or cooking skills are, if you don't like to be in close proximity to people and want a good work–life balance then you'd do well to find another kind of job altogether.

It's also a question of being practical. If you faint at the sight of blood then maybe the medical profession is not for you. And no matter how cool you think you are, there really aren't a lot of professional disc jockeys out there.

Big corporations – a safe bet?

For many years until the latest market meltdown, the most popular career move after graduation was to get into a major corporation – one of those big blue-chip multinationals. From the point of view of a safe place to be, this was the equivalent of winning the lottery. You'd made it, your career was assured.

But it was more than that; it was a place to learn stuff, lots of stuff very quickly. And whatever you did later, it was where, having made the major sale, worked on the mega-project and crunched all those zeros, you gained a grounding that would be forever useful. People looking to transfer from large giants to SMEs, where they may get more autonomy or a chance to be more creative, were usually snapped up because they "knew stuff." They'd been there and done it.

It was also the place, until just a few years ago, where new entrants to the commercial world had access to all the cool technology. Join a Shell or an ExxonMobil, a Philips or a Nokia, a Unilever or a Procter & Gamble and you were assured of having the very best kit there was. That's changed. Now the very smart corporations let their employees bring their own stuff to work and have found ways to integrate it into their systems. That's what's kept Apple shares up and put BlackBerry in trouble. BlackBerry needs expensive servers to work, Apple and many others do not.

So, are large corporations still a good place to learn? Alain Haut is a former senior manager with a series of pharmaceutical firms in France and Switzerland. Now a lecturer at several business schools, he has no doubts that the big company experience is still highly relevant and highly prized today. "I have no doubt that, from a management career perspective, you learn more, much more, much, much more when working for a large corporation," he enthuses. "And this goes for career development, international experience, talent development as well." Haut continues, "Therefore, anything that comes under the heading 'business education and experience' is much better covered in a big corporation." He adds: "Think of it this way, the fundamental courses in business schools the world over are based around the complex environment of the large corporation. That is where the models for business education come from – there is no other one."

Alain Haut's view is strongly supported by search consultant Anthony McAlister: "Whatever your long-term plans may be, experience counts for a lot, probably more than most degrees in the final analysis, so look for large multinational companies that can offer exposure to many different disciplines and become a generalist – never too specialized." He continues: "Good leaders have a broad range of skills that always include learning, influencing, team-working and cross-cultural effectiveness. They also have another thing – common sense. Sadly, that isn't that common in real life!"

But Alain Haut has noticed that there is a definite change in attitude, certainly amongst business school students. The need to get a good job in the big multinationals isn't quite so imperative anymore. Part of the reason, according to McAlister, is the danger that in a big corporation – unless you are very lucky and get put on a fast track – you can become a specialist too soon. As an actor who plays the same character for a long time can become typecast forever, so it is the same with a manager who stays too long in one place doing the same things.

And Haut has also noticed that the business schools – ever on the lookout for new markets to conquer – have moved to attracting ambitious executives from SMEs and even those who want to go it alone as entrepreneurs. But, he says, in reality the model they are teaching hasn't changed: "When I read the course notes for a SME program what do I find, they cover exactly the same ground as the old courses aimed at the multinationals. Maybe they add a little emphasis on innovation – but that's all."

Picking up on McAlister's advice, Haut says that, "Of course, as an entrepreneur, you need to be a generalist. Especially at the beginning when you do all the jobs from CEO down to secretary. So it is important that an entrepreneur starts from the generalist business view, while in large corporations you generally start in a specialist function."

There's little doubt that the big, global corporations will always have plenty of people clamoring at the front door to be allowed in. Equally, there is little doubt that they are great places to learn how a business functions. Their problem is keeping the people they train. Will they do that in the long term, or will the best and brightest, and the not so smart too, drift away to more exciting, innovative opportunities?

Once again, technology is the driver, it is freeing up people to do things in ways that have not been seen before. Virtual, global companies are commonplace, and it is the best and brightest occupying them. But, in the end, what this brings is choice – lots of it. And that can only be a good thing for the worldwide workplace.

The digital driver again

Ben Emmens, a human resources consultant specializing in the aid sector, agrees with Haut and McAlister that to succeed in this complex working world you benefit from some real company experience and certainly it provides that critical grounding that stands anyone in good stead as their career progresses. "I think that to make a portfolio career work, you at least need some workplace experience," says Emmens. "It may not be essential, but I think it makes things a lot easier if you have that kind of corporate experience to draw on. It also gives you a sense of who you are, what you can really do and what you bring to the party."

And this increase in the choice of career, or the ability to mix and match as you want, is, according to Emmens' view, likely not only to continue but increase. "Let's face it," he points out, "people are having two, three or four different careers nowadays and learning opportunities (digital learning) exist to make this ever easier. Neither is it a taboo or a no-no to have more than one job or career." Emmens suggests that it is not just the younger generations who are doing this, but "the drive for all this is coming just as much from the baby boomer generation who still want to have 10 or 20 years' working just like generation X and Y and the Millennials, who don't want to be in the same workforce rut for the next 50 or 60 years."

But, as Emmens is quick to mention, it's the digital emphasis in today's and tomorrow's workplace that is at the heart of much of what happens. Certainly for freelance consultants such as Emmens, it is the digital world that makes doing what he does possible. Because it is a world where he is only as good and only as visible as his digital footprint allows. As he explains, "The last few pieces of work I have won, and the most recent conversations with search and recruitment firms, show how much emphasis is now put on that digital reference and how it now forms a critical part of the due diligence process."

He also refers to those organizations such as Fiverr, Odesk and E-Source: "When you see what they are doing, then the world of work and the organizing, resourcing and procuring of talent look very different from just a few years ago."

How the job search changed

Sandy McLean is a communications professional, with operations in London, Brussels and Washington. She's watched the rise of the social media phenomenon and gives her view of how we have got to where we are today:[1]

> The internet has completely changed the landscape of employment search for job seekers and employers alike. Ten years ago, newspapers and trade magazines were the primary source of job listings – employers advertised and those looking for work searched the printed ads. But as online publishing took off and strangled the advertising lifeline for printed media, publications moved online, too, and offered advertising there. Then specialist online job boards sprang up, usually with advertising. Monster.com was the pioneer over ten years ago in online job postings and is now the leading global online employment solution for job seekers and employers.
>
> Monster Worldwide, Inc. has expanded from being a "job board" to a global provider of a full array of job-seeking, career management, recruitment and talent management products and services. Monster claims that "we are changing the way people think about work, and we're helping them actively improve their lives and their workforce performance with new technology, tools and practices."
>
> Monster also has multiple distribution channels to further extend its reach into local markets in the United States. Harking back to the traditional path for job seekers and employers to meet – the local newspaper – Monster has focused on strategic alliances with newspapers in several of the nation's largest metropolitan markets including New York, Boston, Philadelphia and Chicago.

---

[1] Sandy McLean is the founder of Sandy McLean PR and is a partner of the FutureWork Forum.

> The internet also facilitates remote working and the portfolio career of many consultants, interim workers and freelancers. Many of them joined LinkedIn and other business networking sites online for camaraderie and sources for business. But the further evolution of social media sparked the next revolution in the jobs market (and dramatically changed the whole field of communications).
>
> Many social media sites, especially LinkedIn, Twitter and Facebook, now facilitate job-seeking and employer-vetting. Social media is about communication, but more importantly it is about conversations, not one-way broadcasting, and about branding and relationship-building. Monster talks about "improving the jobseeker experience" through the creation of new products and services, while also "developing deeper relationships with employer customers."

Alexis Grant, a blogger on Mashable, a social network about social media (and about half a dozen other blogging platforms) says: "In this new digital world of work, the era of personal branding and social media and online networking, it's possible to have appealing opportunities fall into your lap – without ever having to beg, or, look for them."

Her tips for using social media to get jobs are:

Showcase your value online with a blog: While developing your online presence is a lot of work, it's the best way to cultivate job offers and other opportunities. A well-done blog also converts first-time visitors into believers of your brand.

Keep your network warm: When we talk about networking, we usually mean meeting new people. But the truth is, keeping the contacts you already have warm can be even more important. If you meet someone and they forget about you the next day, they'll never think of you when a relevant position crosses their desk, even if you're perfect for it. One of the easiest ways to stay top-of-mind is by updating your status on social networks like LinkedIn, Twitter and Facebook. Keep your updates informal and friendly, yet professional, and subtly showcase your value.

Tell people what you're good at: Your contacts will never think of you for a position if they don't know you'd be a great fit. If they do know you have the right skills – and they actually like you – you're a shoo-in.

McLean adds some more advice: "Social media can help job seekers vet employers, and vice versa. LinkedIn is a key tool, but so is Facebook. Potential employers will often check out all social media platforms where a candidate has a presence. This is to protect their reputation as much as to vet candidates. No one wants to hire a racist Twitter ranter, for example. But often employers will also look at grammar, punctuation and use of profanity as filters for vetting prospective employees."

And for employers ...

Sandy McLean continues by explaining how employers can use social networks to improve their recruitment strike rate and build up the reputation of their employment brand:

> First thing to remember is that, while you're chatting away and informing your community of what's going on, you're developing a "social reputation." Social networks are great connectors between organizations and individuals. They act as the common ground, allowing conversations to flow very easily, as both parties understand what to expect from the platform they choose to use. It makes developing relationships very simple and allows you to see further than just the basic business transactions.
>
> The conversations and messages you send through social networks are open for everyone to see, and this is very powerful. Everyone can see how you deal with people and the type of organization you are. Comments people have made to you are displayed and up-to-date. Responses are shown and information is passed transparently for everyone to see. Word of mouth is accelerated. So everything you do creates a reflection of the type of organization you really are. There's nowhere to hide in all this.
>
> My advice is simple: you know your business and the people in it better than anyone, so use what you know to make it as easy as possible for

people to talk to you online, drive conversations, keep relationships fresh and keep everyone up-to-date on your business. This has a greater impact to your organization than driving immediate sales: it builds a trust in your brand, an openness that connects people in a much deeper, more profound way and helps more people understand why your company is the one they should work with.

These are key points for employers to keep in mind to not only attract business/customers, but also to attract the right kind of employees. Nowadays, companies that don't have much of an online presence miss out hugely on opportunities to connect with potential hires, and assess them before they even walk through the door (through their online interactions with the company, or their comments in prospecting emails).

More advice on looking good

It's hard work staying in touch on the social network scene. But hard-pressed job seekers need to do it as an organized part of the waking day. Miriam Salpeter is a social media consultant and the author of *Social Networking for Career Success*.[2] She suggests some more actions that you can do to keep your "face" out there in the marketplace.

"You need to be active on line all the time," she counsels. "Give your opinion and contribute to forums (such as LinkedIn groups) focused on your area of interest. Doing this leaves a trail for recruiters to find when they Google your name. Another thing you can do," she advises, "is use social networking to get to know potential mentors. Join groups and see who is active and may be interested in sharing ideas and suggestions with you."

She also suggests: "Use Twitter, Google+ and Facebook to meet and learn more about people who are seen as thought leaders in your field. Don't hesitate to ask questions, share their posts and comment on what they write. Your goal is to convince new contacts that you are prepared to contribute."

---

[2] Miriam Salpeter, *Social Networking for Career Success*, Learning Express LLC, 2011.

Salpeter goes on to suggest two other ways of keeping your profile out there. "Research how people are searching on LinkedIn for people with the skills you have to offer (www.linkedin.com/skills). Search for your skills and see what buzzwords people are using to describe your work. If it makes sense, add these words to your LinkedIn profile. This will help potential employers find you." The other thing she suggests is that you "use LinkedIn's company pages as a launch pad for your research. It can also help you track down what people working there did before they got that job. Could make a useful link."

Other social media advice

I asked a group of job-seeking graduates for any job-getting tips they had learned while combing the digital recruitment corridors. Employers, you can learn from this too! Here are a few useful ideas:

- Post up good things that happen during your job searches. Praise the would-be employer who actually returned your call, or gave you an interview. News travels, and employees like that.
- Be human, and not too formal. There is a real mix out there in terms of what prospective employers expect from a résumé. When you apply, use the rifle-shot approach not the shotgun. Make it clear that you have researched the company you are applying to.
- Offer to do a trial assignment for free. It is a great way to get in front of people – through the real-life front door. If the company is not local to you, suggest they just email an assignment and you'll do it. It could be a new marketing idea, a design, a product or a service. Either way, neither side has anything to lose.
- Be dogged in your pursuit, but don't overdo it. When does enthusiastic persistence turn into corporate stalking? There's a line somewhere and it is a good idea to know when it is about to be crossed. Upset the prospect and it has all been a waste of time.
- Don't be cute! Some recruiters will tell you to make yourself very visible by just trying to jump out of the herd. Careful! It can go too far. Take out your "silly-ometer" and see if it starts buzzing. Sure you

can "sell the sizzle" as Soshi Games' Cliff Dennett says, but don't go over the top.
- It is also useful to know what's being said about a company before you get to an interview. Check out websites such as www.glassdoor.com, which will give you some useful, unsolicited views of a huge range of employers.

Further advice for job seekers

Having talked up social media as a job seekers paradise, there are others ways of getting hired that also appeal. Certainly if social media is seen as the new way to get a job, looking at some other job-getting strategies from the analogue age may not be a bad idea – even if it's just for a change of pace.

Obviously my Neapolitan voice of youth, Chiara Palieri, whom we heard from in Chapter 1, sees social networking as an important part of the recruitment process – but by no means the only one. She thinks that one of the best ways to get people interested in who you are is to go out and meet them face to face:

> Networking is the key ... Yes, be an avid social media user but also get out there and connect face to face. Make sure to collect business cards and get acquainted with all the businesses you get in touch with ... Read up on as many sources as you can and make sure you keep up-to-date with the latest news and trends in business and technology – they connect people and help you discover incredible opportunities.
>
> Attend as many conferences as you can. Lots of them are free or you can volunteer to help out – it's amazing how many people you can meet this way. I found the best way to find jobs, and meaningful work experience at a high level, was by attending conferences and networking with professionals on LinkedIn. By attending conferences on a regular basis, my network has expanded exponentially. This has given me the invaluable opportunity to connect with people whose acquaintance marked a real turning point in my professional career.

Finally, she also advises: "Keep the balance between formal and informal education. Remember, you need creativity and an enterprising spirit to get a job nowadays."

Atanaska Varbanova of Think Young in Brussels agrees with Palieri:

> Nowadays information is everywhere and all you need to do is not let that escape your sight. This does not mean that it is enough to sit and wait until opportunities come along. Being proactive is more than ever the key to getting hired. Staying connected with the right people, in the right networks, keeping your profile visible is part of the challenge of today's "connected generation". There are so many new opportunities, not only to find interesting work, but also to volunteer and find new interests. And you never know when one of these could take you into your dream job.

Take every opportunity

When it comes to getting a job or choosing a career, that balance between formal and informal, as Palieri terms it, may just be the deciding factor. Aaron White works for the Center for Creative Leadership (CCL), one of the world's leading providers of leadership training and development. CCL is headquartered in Greensboro, North Carolina, with offices around the world. White has found himself in probably CCL's most exotic outpost, Addis Ababa, the capital of Ethiopia. From there, White travels extensively, working with many local African communities and using leadership techniques to improve how people structure and organize their lives. White is a firm believer that while the digital revolution can help, it's your personal drive and character that will get you employed. Here are some insightful thoughts from White on building a career:

> My experience has been that to make things happen it takes a bit of luck (seeing serendipitous moments as opportunities and being at the right place at the right time) and the willingness to say "yes" to new opportunities. When I look back at some of the adventurous experiences I've had, most have come about because I

> was able to recognize a unique opportunity and say "yes," without fully understanding the outcome, or sometimes the consequences, of that choice. I think a lot of people are too scared to get out of their comfort zone and because of that miss out on a lot of rich opportunities.
>
> Like many people my age, my educational background relates little to what I do in my job. Three things that have definitely helped me in my work have been: an ability to relate to people from different cultures, the ability to write in a coherent manner, and digital media skills. Combining these skills has allowed me to take a more entrepreneurial path to get where I am, but is also of personal interest to me so working with these have come naturally. For anyone interested in working in international development but don't have the experience, I would recommend that they start traveling to less developed countries to get some exposure to the work/life/culture. Masters degrees in a related field is [sic] also helpful, but the drive and willingness to get outside your comfort zone is far more impressive to employers.

Aaron White continues by suggesting that many people seeking jobs need to be much more active in linking up with real people if they want to succeed in their job search and build a successful and fulfilling career:

> I think a lot of young people looking for work don't move far enough away from their computers to meet the right people and get the right experiences that would set them up for success. I have a friend who moved to New York looking for a job, but then spent the next three months holed up in a micro-studio-apartment sending out his résumé to 50+ companies and waiting for a reply. He eventually left New York without a job and without any money. In contrast, another friend – a budding photographer – went to New York and went straight to the National Geographic offices, talking his way in to meet an editor. Within two days of being in New York he was able to start an internship that eventually led to a great job. So, my advice is to get off these job websites and to go meet real people. Never

underestimate the value of human interactions and the opportunities to develop relationships. Say "yes" to jobs that don't pay in order to do something you enjoy, or to get the experience you need. Do the good work and the reward you need will follow.

... AND DON'T FORGET THE CAMELS!

Getting out there and just doing it as the Center for Creative Leadership's Aaron White suggests can lead to all sorts of adventures and outcomes. But I thought that this was so "over the top cool" that it had to be mentioned here: Aaron owns camels in Ethiopia. Not a lot of young people from North Carolina can say that, can they? Here's the story. Let it be a lesson that getting out and talking with people, rather than hiding behind a screen all day, is a much more fun option:

> I worked for a season among nomadic Somali camel herders in the far corner of Ethiopia. It was incredibly difficult work managing several humanitarian aid projects in drought-afflicted communities, but also very rewarding. I became close with my Somali "uncle," Mohammed Yusuf, who kept me out of trouble, taught me about the local culture, and instilled in me a great respect for camels. We spent a lot of time drinking camel milk and sometimes eating roasted camel meat. As nomadic pastoralists, the life of many Somalis revolves around the camel and a high regard is held for their resiliency and ability to sustain themselves in the harsh conditions and provide nutrition through milk. In Somalia they're like a bank account. So you would never ask how many camels a person owns, just like I would never ask how much money you make. Because of my close connection with the community and my interest in camels, I was given two male camels as a gift. This is quite a big honor (and worth nearly $2,000, which is a lot of money to these people), and although I don't exactly know where my camels reside (they're off with a herd of camels in the desert), I'm still able to hold my connection to that community. I suppose you could say that it's my emergency backup if I go bankrupt and need to start over! Although if I were a better camel manager I would sell off my camels (or

> trade) for females, growing my herd and my status. The camels' names are George and Abdi.
>
> I hope you enjoyed that story. It just goes to show what can happen when you give yourself some room to move. Also I have now won my bet that I could work a camel story into the book!

And a few tips of my own

Over the years, I've spent a lot of time helping people find employment: young people seeking their first real job, those in mid-career who need to change and people at the end of their careers who are not ready to hang up their hat (or keyboard) just yet:

- First, as Aaron White suggested, you've got to get out there and mix it. You'll never get a job sitting at home staring at a screen. Go and see people, and find excuses to do that.
- Always look for the less obvious pathway. The obvious routes are very well trodden; what you need is something that will give you an edge.
- Don't be afraid to ask advice or get someone to talk through your ideas with. And this applies to anyone of any age.
- If you can, try and make yourself an expert at something. It's amazing just how easily this can be done. Many years ago I was asked to do a study about women in the workplace. After it was published (with my name on it) the report became a huge (short-lived!) hit. Suddenly I was in demand as a speaker on women in the workplace. Two months earlier, I knew nothing, now I was being touted as "the global expert on women's employment."
- The thing to learn from that is that when these things happen, whether by design or just serendipitous accident, go with the flow. The adventure is usually interesting.
- This is not about young people. Everyone can have fun. I know of many 50–60-year-olds who have used their experience to carve

out exciting new careers. It's all a question of linking creativity to determination.
- The age thing is interesting and offers new opportunities. I work (I'm in my 60s) with a lot of younger people (in their 20s, 30s and 40s). It's terrific fun and I find that I learn as much from them as they learn from me.

"USE THE PHONE? – ARE YOU CRAZY?"

Life has finally caught up with all those first-time job seekers who grew up texting and then tweeting their every thought. Recruiters have noticed that this young generation has one big skill missing – the ability to talk on the phone. They'll text, even email, anyone, but they don't feel comfortable actually talking to someone. This is a bit of a problem when you are offering a service or trying to sell something. Here's a tip. If you want to get a job, get some practice making calls. We may live in the digital age, but communication skills – talking to people – are still very vital in most occupations. Remember Aaron White's advice earlier?

More tips for job-seeking graduates

Here are a few other ideas to keep those job-hunting first-timers on their toes:

- Have a realistic idea of what you're qualified for. Too many college students come out of school without understanding what jobs they have a realistic shot at being able to succeed at. As a result, they often aim too high and then get frustrated when they don't get interviews. Make sure to talk to people in the profession you'd like to enter in order to understand how best to frame your candidacy and what jobs to target first.
- Don't put too much detail about your course work on your résumé. Recent grads spend the first half of their résumé on education, notes on course work and honors. But what you really want to

play up is work experience, not details about your courses. A hiring manager is likely to spend only 20 seconds on the initial scan of your résumé and what he or she needs to see in that time is work experience directly relevant to what he or she's hiring for, not a list of college courses you took. Remember to "sell the sizzle!"

- Think about it, when you're right out of school, you rarely have enough work experience to justify a résumé longer than one page – and it can make you come across as self-important or unable to edit. Stick to a single page if your experience is limited – but make what you have done interesting. Also you're most unlikely to be qualified for your dream job straight out of school, and holding out for one will make you lose out on other opportunities. More importantly, you really can't know whether something is a dream job or not until you're working there. While you might think that you might love doing that work for that company, it might turn out that the boss is a nightmare, or your co-workers are horrible. In reality, dream jobs can be just that – a dream.

BEING SQUEAKY CLEAN

With so much open communication it is all too easy these days for your sins to find you out. Stories abound of usually soberly behaved guys and gals having a few too many in some exotic resort and foolishly pasting the photographic results on their Facebook page. So, as more and more would-be employers ask to see (or take a peek without permission) social media pages, are there any hard and fast rules we should take heed of?

Communications professional Sandy McLean, who runs a public relations firm with offices in London, Washington and Brussels, says that "a good idea for prospective employees is to review their 'social' pages from the point of view of an employer and consider closing down sites that don't show you in the best light." She advises that updates to social networks like LinkedIn, Twitter and Facebook should be informal and friendly – yet professional. "That's relatively easy to remember for LinkedIn," McLean says, "because it is a professional platform. But for many people, Twitter, Facebook and other social media platforms fall into the personal, 'fun' category and are not the focus of scrupulous attention to reputation."

Without putting your social media status into the totally boring, not-worth-a-look category, here are Sandy McLean's tips for keeping out there but pleasing a would-be employer or client:

- Try to avoid making disparaging comments about employers or co-workers, even if you think your pages are only open to people you trust – the social media is one big leaky boat.
- It's NEVER a good idea to use bad language on social media.
- Regularly review and edit friends and followers. Would you be embarrassed for your employee or a prospective boss or client to see their comments? If so, de-friend or block them, or at least hide them.
- Avoid posting, sharing or "liking" photos or images in bad taste.
- If you are determined to have political discussions, keep the tone of your comments even-handed and non-aggressive. Avoid joining group discussions for extreme groups or causes.

McLean has this additional advice, which is worth adopting: "I use LinkedIn and Twitter for business, but reserve Facebook for keeping in touch with far-flung family and friends," she says. "My overarching rule is, 'What would Mother think?', since she is one of my Facebook friends and sees my posts. She's moved on somewhat from her straight-laced, Southern lady days, but she still holds her children to high standards of good manners, grammar and language."

Good advice indeed! To hark back to the email age, let's add one more. The rule of thumb used to be "never put in an email what you wouldn't like to see in the *New York Times*."

What I need to do better

Communication professional Adam Bentham says that one of the things he struggles with is how to get across his point of view regarding an effective workplace to other – often more senior – colleagues. This, for him, is particularly frustrating when it comes to old ways of working bumping up against the new. And he says that there are two specific things he'd like to know, if someone would like to write in and tell him.

"First," he explains, "I would greatly benefit from having the tools to win the argument for flexible working and home-working. Why? Because I need to persuade senior management and CEOs that for me to be most effective I am much more productive working on a Mac book somewhere with good Wi-Fi." He continues, "Right now in my current job that just doesn't happen. I am in an office environment where I am constantly disturbed to help out colleagues because I know the ropes and have been in the job longer than them."

Bentham raises a good point. Enlightened bosses need to review work practices. There is no doubt today that there is more than one way of getting the job done. Certainly a lot of the ways we work are detrimental to productivity.

Bentham's other point is also highly relevant: "What languages should I and my fellow workers be learning to be ready for the workspace of the future and be most desirable to employers?" Well that probably depends on what your career plans are and where you want to go or what type of industry you want to work in. Establish that first, then if Mandarin or Japanese, Russian or Spanish will assist you in your goals, take it from there.

> **IT'S NOT ABOUT YOU!**
>
> If you want to get a job – or even get an interview – you'd better learn a few basics very quickly. Too many job seekers fail to get over the first hurdle because they just don't know how to sell what they have to offer.
>
> Cliff Dennett is the founder and CEO of Soshi Games, a start-up online games firm based in Birmingham. Soshi employs 15

people (most of them first-time job seekers), so he knows what works and what doesn't when it comes to getting hired.

"People still get their CVs all wrong," Dennett laments. "In the past, the main gripe I had about CVs was the poor spelling and grammar. Although that is still a problem (and quickly disqualifies a large number of people), spell-checker technology has solved a lot of that. But now the biggest problem is that the applications they send in are all about THEM, not what they will do for ME and my organization."

He continues: "The vast majority of cover letters I get are all about what they are looking for and what they will get out of the job. I don't care (actually, I do, but not in the first instance). As a cash-strapped start-up trying to move as fast as possible, I want to know what that person will do for us."

Dennett adds: "The tone of the letters usually says, 'I want to work with you, because you can help me achieve ...' They have obviously done no research on us and the letter is one of hundreds they have sent out. These go straight into the e-bin!"

According to Dennett, the next mistake is emphasizing the wrong things:

> All the CVs I get from people straight out of education – whether school or university – all begin with their academic achievements. This is definitely NOT the most important thing for me ... What I want to know, right up front, is what have you done and what kind of person are you. I want to be able to feel the sizzle!

> Even the good CVs don't really have much of a clue how to sell the "sizzle" of the things they have done – even if it's just running the student bar at college. Personally, I think this is the result of a drop in focus on the arts in schools ... And if I've spent my childhood years adopting different personas and projecting myself to an audience in school plays, I bet I can sell myself better ... If I've had to come up with original ideas, whether in music, art or dance, then I've probably had to think through what other people might want and adapt my style to them. I see none of this in the CVs I get.

Taking the entrepreneurial route

Peter Vogel is a serial entrepreneur. At just 29 he has already started a series of businesses from online job matching to teaching rich young Saudi Arabians how to get a work ethic. Vogel is convinced that the current tough economic climate, coupled with the rapid emergence of the digital world, has opened the way to more entrepreneurs, making it easier to get started.

He is joined in that belief by Soshi Games' founder Cliff Dennett, who adds: "I think there is a general mistrust of the big corporations. However, there is also the rise of the celebrity CEO (Zuckerberg at Facebook, Pincus at Zyngna, Brin at Google) who have made being boss of a start-up cool again." He continues: "I also think that there have been a lot of redundancies across many industries and I talk to people who don't want to have some faceless corporation having that power over them again. They'd rather be in control of their own destinies."

Most valuable trait for an entrepreneur

Vogel says that for him, "persistence is a key element. Often people give up too quickly." But he adds quickly, "another important factor is the team – or the people you can have around you to advise. No one can be an expert in everything, therefore having people who complement your own abilities is vital."

Cliff Dennett more or less agrees, but says, "Undoubtedly the number one trait is tenacity. You have to completely and utterly believe that what you are doing is going to work." He comments that "every day you expect a leap of progress and often it is only a small step. I know from my own experiences how things never, ever worked out the way you'd hoped." He explains how "All the planning, strategizing and execution in the world cannot prepare the first-time entrepreneur for this. So, the only thing that can get you through is tenacity."

Another serial entrepreneur is Jens Maier. After a stellar corporate career that included senior positions in the automotive and finance industries, he has been involved in start-ups and is also much in demand as a lecturer in business strategy and innovation at business schools such as Cranfield, the London Business School and St Gallen.³

Maier thinks that "understanding and leveraging what you are really good at" is the key, but adds that "you need to be able to move fast, think holistically and in networks and, above all, be comfortable with yourself outside the security of that corporate hierarchy."

This, says Maier, is where a lot of corporate folk go wrong. They just can't make that transition. "You can only make it on your own if you are able to fully exploit both your personal network and your corporate network."

"Believe in yourself," advises Sunita Malhotra, a corporate coach and mentor based in Brussels, "too many people seem to think that they are forced to go work for themselves and don't really believe in it. That way they will never succeed."

Stay optimistic

Malhotra advises would-be entrepreneurs to "stay optimistic. Keep your ears and eyes open for all opportunities. Business comes out of the most unlikely places. You meet someone and they become a friend, then suddenly an opportunity opens up. Don't forget that getting business can take a very long time these days. You can take 18 months to two years from giving a pitch to getting the business."

The other thing Malhotra counsels is, "Don't expect to continue the luxury of corporate life. No more assistants booking your travel, sitting in the front of the plane, expense account eating. So, you must be able to face reality. And you've got to be able to multitask. By that I mean talk to a client one minute, then take out the garbage! Know how to build great networks, and never stop doing that. Ideally be networked long before you need to use it to generate business."

---

³ Jens Maier was awarded the Best Teaching Award 2012, HSG Diplom Programm für Technologie Unternehmer at the University of St Gallen, Switzerland. He is a partner of the FutureWork Forum.

Generating business is what Cliff Dennett sees as a major skill. And he lists three more top attributes that he says are equally critical to building success as an entrepreneur.

"To be able to sell. And I mean to customers, the banks, investors, employees – your wife! Everyone needs to believe in what you are doing, because if they don't your support network collapses." He continues, "For people to be supportive they have to believe and for that, the entrepreneur has to be able to sell."

"To be able to hold conflicting versions of the future in your head and be happy with all of them." And he explains that "Entrepreneurs need to be able to flex, listen to others and act, often in directions they are not sure of, or not comfortable with. Often you have to step outside of your own emotions, really listen to others, swallow some pride and get on with it."

"But there's one more, that for me is very important," Dennett says, which is "to be able to say, 'I don't know that' and then go and find out (or employ) someone who does." He explains that "all the stakeholders need to have faith in you that you know what you are doing, even if privately they think you are stark staring mad. But the faith is vital, that you know what you are doing, so sometimes you have to find out stuff very fast to keep that going."

The power of persuasion

Jens Maier has similar views, even if his emphasis is slightly different.

"What I wish I'd had a lot more of is the ability to persuade people. And particularly how to influence without power. That's one of the things an entrepreneur needs to succeed, being able to get people to do things when you can't order them as their boss." And Maier adds four other things that he'd like to have in his entrepreneur's arsenal of attributes: "clarity – making complex things simple; humility (most entrepreneurs aren't good at that); dealing with ambiguity; and, finally, winning the hearts and minds of followers."

Ever practical, and speaking like the engineer he is by education, Peter Vogel had this to say about required skills: "I personally never attended a single business class in my life. However, I had an excellent coach who really helped me advance the business." He concludes: "Certainly, a bit of business education could have done me good, but I am convinced that the most critical things can only be learned by doing them."

Cliff Dennett raised one more critical issue – money. "The other thing I have experienced is the 'emotion' of discovering where money really comes from! This was sadly missing from the MBA modules I took. Until it happened, I didn't even think about the added emotional pressure of having investors 'money' (much of it from personal friends) to spend. It is an interesting experience and not perhaps for everyone."

Maybe some of Dennett's concerns color Jens Maier's final remark: "I am moving around the European, Anglo-Saxon and Asian worlds and the emphasis varies considerably. But, I'd like to say this: for me Continental Europe stands out. Sadly, the public debate centers far too much on what the state or government can do for you." And he gives an example: "Take social networks. Everyone is connected all the time. OK, that's fun and everyone is active. But there is a paradox here. If no one is sitting on their hands and we are all busy, why do we not see thousands of businesses springing up? What's the story, individuals versus government; having fun, versus making money?"

Maybe it depends where you are. Patrick Faniel of the UBIS business school in Geneva recently visited a business school in Poland, where one-third of the graduating class had firm plans to set up their own companies.But if all these would-be job seekers and entrepreneurs are going to make it, they will need a few other attributes in their "how-to-get-hired" toolkit. How they interview is right at the top. What kind of first impression do you make?

Making an impression

There's that old saying, "you never get a second chance to make a first impression." The fact is that it is still a good saying to keep in mind.

One of the things that are extremely important to get right if you are off to an interview is to have some idea of what they expect you to look like when you show up. Now there aren't many places these days that expect the suit, white shirt and sober tie. But it isn't a bad idea to know that you are not going to stand out when you arrive for your interview. The other thing here is that, how an organization dresses very much sums up its culture. So you can get some really good ideas about what it would be like to work there, just by logging on to their website and looking at the people they feature.

Khalid Aziz is the founder of his eponymous organization that specializes in presentation and leadership development. He is based in Winchester in the UK and has spent many years counseling leading CEOs, statesmen and politicians on how to present themselves.

So, is it true you never get a second chance to make that first impression?

> There is a school of thought that people make some pretty in-depth decisions about you within the first half-second of meeting you. Quite often this is based on negatives. Most people when interviewing candidates for a job have, as it were, a switch which has a default position of "How can I not hire this person?" In other words, they are trying to minimize the risk of hiring the wrong person as that will reflect badly on them. As an interviewee you have to work hard at flipping that switch to "How can I get this person on board?" First impressions that are negative, mean you have a much higher mountain to climb so try and minimize any "reasons not to buy." I am afraid this means a tendency towards conservatism but remember people usually appoint people in their own image. So if they have a casual T-shirt dress-down policy there is probably little point in turning up in a three-piece pinstripe suit!

What about other kinds of interviews, such as video or Skype? Here, too, Aziz has some useful thoughts. "The key thing is not to get too relaxed," he explains. "If you're doing a Skype interview from the comfort of your home you run the risk of allowing yourself to be too comfortable and you might not be at your sharpest. You may not be dressed as well as you might if you were turning up physically for an interview and that can have an effect too."

But Aziz notes that "one of the positives about a Skype interview is that the delays can offer you more chance to think about answers to probing questions. No one will mind if you pause that little bit longer; they'll put it down to broadband delays. The biggest challenge is getting through two pieces of glass – the camera lens on your computer and the screen at the other end. There are no easy solutions to this apart from the time-honoured advice from photographers – 'Make love to the camera!'"

Aziz has more advice on creating a CV that sizzles: it should be "short and tailored to the job specification." And he warns: "Beware of including wacky extracurricular activities. Not everyone will appreciate you being into extreme ironing. Wherever possible always run your CV past someone of the same age group as the interviewer. They will often spot egregious entries that will have your CV heading for the round file on the floor."

Does he have any useful anecdotes about interviewing that may help the reader? "It's always dangerous to overclaim on your CV. One interviewee made great play of their two years in Hong Kong where they 'picked up the local lingo' to an interviewer who was clearly a British-born mother-tongue English speaker. Little did he know that he was a linguist with a first from Oxford. He soon discovered the pitfalls of overclaiming when the interviewer immediately switched into Cantonese for the rest of the interview! If all else fails, try honesty!"

LOOKING GOOD, LANDING A JOB

Susan Huskisson is the founder and president of Speechworks, and one of the world's leading presentation skills coaches. She is based in Marbella, Spain and numbers many of the Fortune 500 companies as clients.[4] After a lengthy career in America, where she wrote speeches for US presidents, she then transferred her talents to Europe. Using the background of her best-selling book as a basis, here she provides a primer on how to get hired, how to present and how to get on in the business world.

YOU'RE HIRED!

One of my clients told me about a young man they recently asked to make a presentation for his job interview. The candidate arrived at the corporate offices, connected his laptop with his PowerPoint presentation to the projector, and proceeded to watch the slide show, sitting with the audience. In his mind, a presentation meant putting PowerPoint on the screen. He missed a big opportunity to present *himself* to the panel (he didn't get the job – surprise, surprise). What speakers often forget is that THEY are the message – not the slides.

Standing or sitting in front of any audience (senior managers, the Board, peers, customers) with confidence is increasingly important in getting the job, keeping it and advancing. Whether the presentation is one-to-one, a job interview or to a large audience, voice, body language, and the ability to articulate the important points in a logical and concise way will help anyone get to where he or she wants to go professionally. So how do we make the good "first impression" and keep that lasting impression when we meet or present to other people?

GETTING THE JOB

Consider the job interview, what is the first nonverbal signal you give the interviewer? Are you on time (or a bit early)? Your punctuality is the first impression you make. Maybe you should get a taxi (early) that day instead of dealing with public

---

[4] Susan Huskisson is the author of *Easy Eloquence*, Long Acre Press, 2009, and a partner of the FutureWork Forum.

transportation and possible delays. You want to arrive feeling unstressed and unruffled.

How are you dressed? Wear something that is appropriate for the job you are seeking, perhaps a bit dressier. If you want an IT job where everyone wears jeans and T-shirts, save that combo for when you get the job. Wear something a bit more professional for the interview, you may be meeting someone other than the IT person. Shine the shoes, be careful of any jewelry that might be distracting (dangling earrings), be neat (nicely laundered shirts, hair tidy, etc.) and make sure the clothes are comfortable. How you *feel* in the clothes may be just as important as how you *look* in them.

Those first moments are critical. Do you smile, have good eye contact, posture and a firm handshake? Yes? So far, so good. You have just made another nice first impression. Carry as little with you as possible since you don't want to be balancing papers, bags, purses. You might bring your CV with you but try not to give it to the interviewer until you are leaving. You want that person to look at YOU – not the paper.

Your body language during the interview will be observed. Movements should have purpose (no jittering or playing with hair!). If you have more than one interviewer, try to look at all of them, not just the person asking the question, when you respond. Don't leave anyone out!

Voice is important as well – good volume and enunciation, energy, enthusiasm as you speak are vital.

Prepare answers to questions you believe you may receive so you will have strong responses. For instance, if you have experience or training that will be valuable for the job you want, be sure to identify your strengths before the session, and then find the right time to tell the interviewer what you have done. And think about your weaknesses for that job too. Be prepared to deal with questions you would rather not have – even better, think about pre-empting the negative questions by addressing them before you are asked (if you are sure the issue will arise) and have solid (truthful) answers that will benefit you. For instance, you may not have experience in one area, so you might comment early in the interview on some ability you have that might be even more important.

Some people are better at interviewing than others. The ones who interview well are those who seem confident (we are back to the body language and voice!). They have done their homework, so they know what kinds of questions to ask about the job and the company – and perhaps about the person who is doing the interview. The ability to ask questions in an interview may be as important as the skill of answering them. The more you can get the interviewer to talk, the smarter they think you are! When answering questions, give ample thought in advance to key messages you want to make, then look for opportunities to express these ideas in response to questions. And no matter how awful your current employer is, NEVER, NEVER criticize! While you may be absolutely correct in your assessment of the people/company where you work, interviewers take a dim view of job applicants who bad mouth their current or past organizations.

Job interviews often require the interviewee to make a presentation, because companies know that this speaking skill will be important in the future. Senior managers don't have time to read reports – they expect the condensed oral version from their employees. Speakers who can present accurate, succinct material to senior management will be welcome in boardrooms across the globe. Remember, unless you are hired to prepare PowerPoint shows, the stage belongs to YOU, not the screen. If you must use slides, start from the center of the stage with a blank screen for your introduction, go to the slides, and blank them again for your closing (with you in the center again). The most important attention-getting moments in the presentation are for you, not the slides.

TECHNOLOGY

With the use of electronic communication, the verbal and nonverbal skills we have discussed become even more important.

When the transmission involves video, cameras can magnify subtle movements; when the transmission involves only voice, vocal projection has great impact. Surprisingly, good voice involves good body language. Posture and correct breathing have an impact on vocal quality. Standing up when you speak on the telephone helps your voice project more authority. Early radio presenters always stood – and they wore formal attire to help them feel more professional. The listener can hear the "smile" in your voice if you actually smile when speaking. And remember that body language is very visible when we are listening to others during video web conferences. We are not invisible because we are not speaking. Looking attentive – watching the person who is talking, using confident posture, hands on the table – will give a good impression to viewers.

Clothes and jewelry can be important on video as well. Avoid clothes with patterns (tweed, herringbone, stripes, checks) that can "move" on camera. Save the large, shiny, dangling jewelry for later since it does not play well on camera. Consider your backdrop when choosing colors to wear; a charcoal/red/burgundy jacket can look nice with a light-colored wall behind you, while a pastel jacket can make you fade into the background. And stay away from strong contrasts (white shirt and black jacket, for instance) that tend to drain color away from your face. Pull your hair back so the viewer can see you. Hair tumbling over the eyes can be distracting (for you and the observer). If you use eye glasses, wear non-reflective lenses so the lights do not create a glare (and block the feeling of eye contact).

On video, look at the camera for the most part when you are talking. That gives people on the other side the feeling you are looking at them. Hopefully your video camera is located directly over the viewing screen, but sometimes it isn't.

SOCIAL MEDIA

The good news is that social media makes it easy for us to reach many people instantaneously. The bad news is that social media makes it easy to reveal to the world – instantaneously – our shortcomings and mistakes. The online employment website CareerBuilder estimates that 37 percent of companies that are hiring use social media sites to research job applicants (65 percent of these use Facebook). A night out with friends and too much to drink may not be the image you want your prospective boss to see on your Facebook page. In the CareerBuilder study, one-third of the hiring managers said they had found information on the website that prevented them from hiring the applicant (including drinking, drug use, criticism of current employer, or just plain poor writing skills). Yes, these sites are supposed to be private, but companies manage to find out a great deal anyway. Before posting material that is questionable, give serious thought as to how your boss (or the person you hope to be your boss) would react if they saw it. If in doubt – DON'T!

THE CV THAT SELLS

Your CV can be your emissary to the organization before you meet anyone in the hiring group. That (hopefully) short, one-page summary of your life should be the "teaser" that makes them want to know more about you. Clearly and **briefly** identifying your career goals, previous experience (show results of your work and tailor this part for the job you are seeking), education and training, awards or recognition, and any particularly interesting personal information (hobbies, etc.) that will help you get the interview for the job can be included. You might leave out the potentially dangerous hobbies (like skydiving or bungee jumping) that could be considered too risky! Don't elaborate or add details. If you can keep the résumé to one page (maximum two) your CV is more likely to be read. Lengthy documents are put aside. Remember, the CV is there for you to get your foot in the door, not to get you the job. No one has time to read the details. Think "elevator pitch" here.

Jackie Merckx, a former head of Human Resources for many international organizations, recommends information in the following order:

- Job Objectives
- Experience
- Education
- Personal Statement and Other Information

Remember, the shorter – the better. In this case less is most certainly more.

HOW TO GET HIRED

What better way to learn how to land a job than take the up-to-the-minute advice of someone who's just been there, done that and got the T-shirt. Amrit Thind studied in Switzerland and then attended university in the UK. During his initial job searches after graduation, he got so frustrated with the kind of responses to his applications that he and his friends made a much viewed YouTube video about it, titled "Lost in Application." A project that coincidently helped him land his first job![5] Early in the research and planning for this book, I gave Amrit Thind a challenge. Talk to your friends and build up a checklist for landing a job. This is his report. It's worth taking note, because it is grounded in the realities of the marketplace and is full of good advice and common sense.

AMRIT THIND'S CHECKLIST TO LAND THE JOB YOU WANT

Know your industry: you aren't just looking for a job, but rather the best match for your skill set and experience.[6] It's important to know where you want to begin searching so that you can gauge

---

[5] You can view the video at www.youtube.com/watch?v=j6Kg7eq7CIs.
[6] http://www.washingtonpost.com/jobs_articles/how-to-stand-out/2012/10/09/635c9e72-124d-11e2-be82-c3411b7680a9_story.html.

whether you are a suitable fit for the industry, or industries, you are looking into, or so that you can tailor your skills to that industry. It could be the case you have skills you didn't know would be applicable, but thinking about them in the context of that industry is beneficial. Make sure you don't only know about one industry. Know about them all. This will expand your understanding of the workplace and the different industries out there. Read the *Financial Times* and know what's going on ...

... and know who won't hire you: You may not yet have the required skills or experience, your personality might not align with their company culture, or your salary expectations could be too high. For a number of reasons, some organizations simply won't hire you. Know these organizations and don't waste your time on them if the chances for success are low or zero to start with.

Do your research: tailor your application to the company you are applying to and do not sound generic. Too many people send bland, catch-all résumés that could relate to any company, and they send their applications around without putting much effort into cover letters. Employers want to recruit somebody who really wants to work for them and has made an effort. Do your research, most of which can be done on a company website or Google. It is crucial to tailor and hammer home to the recruiter that you know exactly what the company does, why they are special and what their niche might be. Don't get it wrong. If you try to target the company but at the expense of sounding ignorant – for instance using out-of-date examples of their work – your application will most likely not be successful. And remember, it is not what you want, it's what you are offering them (see earlier advice from Soshi Games' Cliff Dennett).

Don't present yourself as a finished product: employers welcome it when people show themselves as dynamic, changing and in progress. You do not need to tell them everything you don't know yet, but it is good to let them know that you are applying to their company because you want to learn X, Y and Z by working there.

Relate what you want to learn to the research you have conducted. Show off your unfinished work and what you are passionate about. Not everything you create has to have been in a classroom or in the professional world, or even "finished." Depending on where you are applying, try to show something practical that relates to the industry. Prove that you are seriously interested in working for the company and make a considered application.

(Depending on the company) do not limit your personality to a two-page CV: after thinking about the industry and your matching skill sets you can move on to thinking about the right way of approaching a company. Even if you're not looking to work within a creative industry, it could be invaluable to consider novel or creative approaches – or at least step away from the standardized, chronological CV. Find a better way to showcase your personality. It's all about showing how you're a good fit for their company, and there personality, above experiences, can play a key role. Can you create an online résumé, use social media, or build an infographic about yourself?[7]

Not all companies care if your CV runs on longer than two pages if it is a bit more creative in what you include. You can create a CV that shows more about yourself than just sentences and facts. The world of online social media allows for people to apply this way. However, for applications that fall out of the norm, job seekers often approach them with a mental block, feeling the pressure to be creative and use different techniques. Use whatever mix sells and suits you naturally as a person – do not force it. Sell your personality and try to bring your personal projects, passions and ambitions to life.

Here are some examples of creative applications:

- An application that looks like an Amazon page: http://www.phildub.com/

---

[7] http://www.forbes.com/sites/theyec/2013/04/25/how-to-stand-out-in-a-crowded-job-market-forget-the-traditional-resume/.

- A self-promotion video of a copywriter who had just moved to London looking for employment: https://www.youtube.com/watch?v=Kb-UdRa0Vaw
- A speculative job inquiry from Graeme Anthony: http://wearesocial.net/blog/2010/09/job-application/
- A young graduate addressing some of the problems students face when looking for jobs in an environment of austerity and unemployment. Rumor has it he was subsequently recruited by NASA and is currently in the process of inventing the next internet : https://www.youtube.com/watch?v=j6Kg7eq7CIs

Social media is good, but optimize your application: it's great if you've made a website or turned your Twitter feed into a résumé, BUT a problem may arise when trying to process an application if it needs to be printed and distributed. Optimize and tailor your application for the company you are applying to (it's important to show that this has been created for them alone). There is no one size fits all. Whilst it is good to use social media, do not overtly rely on using videos and websites. Instead, include it as a healthy mix in your overall application.

Your cover letter is crucial: a short, well-written cover letter is THE big thing. Make sure your cover letter doesn't just highlight why you are applying for the job and what would make you a good fit for the company. A cover letter must also look professional and be presented like a letter. Create a signature for your emails and pay attention to formatting and layout. We live in the 21st century – display your competence with technology and design. Simple formatting and visual appeal make a cover letter something a recruiter will want to read as opposed to an application immediately dismissed.[8]

And remember, as Cliff Dennett of Soshi Games points out, learn how to "sell the sizzle"!

---

[8] http://mashable.com/2013/05/12/job-different/.

Make no mistakes: this should go without saying, but sadly far too many CVs have fatal errors in them (fatal in the fact that you won't get a job even if you are the next Einstein). Any mistake – ranging from the smallest typo to getting the name of your potential employer wrong – can cost you a job.

Be dogged: applications can be incredibly frustrating because employers will often not get back to you. Be dogged. Send emails and follow-up emails. "Like" the company on Facebook, find your recruiter on LinkedIn or Google Plus – know everything about them. Build up contacts and relationships in the industry you are interested in. Leave messages, attend and volunteer at industry- or company-related events. Most importantly, make an impression. Make sure you are remembered. Ask for relevant contact details and try to set up a meeting. Often it is far more effective to ask for career advice rather than a job explicitly. This gives you the opportunity to flaunt your personality rather than hone in on a job like a vulture on its prey.

Network, network, network (that's your mantra): network with anyone, everyone, everywhere, all the time, online, offline. Look for connections all the time, even where you think there aren't any. Build the connections that already exist (even if they have the potential to be a dead end). Realize that your network starts at home. Parents, relatives and friends can all provide ideas and advice and contacts, if not a job. Engage with the industry at any level, display your passion and drive to be involved, and be part of that industry.[9]

Know yourself and go niche: do you have experience and skills that can help you to get a foot into niche roles? Embark on a search to find niche job boards dedicated to the industry you want to work within. These sites give access to listings that aren't advertised on larger job boards, meaning there are smaller applicant pools and less competition.[10] They also have

---

[9] http://blog.brazencareerist.com/2013/02/26/10-powerful-ways-to-stand-out-as-a-job-seeker/.
[10] http://mashable.com2013/01/06/stand-out-job-search-2013/.

the potential to build direct connections with the people who may be hiring in future. More niche plus less people equals more chances to network with those that matter.

Start a company instead of writing a résumé: don't be afraid to start your own business – even if the likelihood of it being successful is slim. Market yourself as a founder and visionary, a self-starter and hard-worker. Being proactive and showing initiative can be more effective than sending out hundreds of applications. Large companies often operate through acquisition strategies, buying up smaller ones not only for their products but also for their employees.[11]

Amrit Thind is still working toward his ideal job, but he is employed and has – using the techniques outlined above – been very successful in carving out a promising career.

One of the things I liked most about Amrit's ideas was that they looked at non-direct ways of getting in front of prospective employers. Here's another that I've used (more specifically for client development, but the idea is the same).

What you do is start a research project. That's easy, no one knows you, so give it an imposing name and also your organization that is going to be doing the research (one guy I know actually gave himself the title of Chief Scientist! – now that's a really cool idea even if you don't know one end of a Bunsen burner from another). Then what you do is hit the phones and ask to come in and meet key people in organizations and ask them questions. If you can get your college or university on side with this, it helps with the credibility factor. These days, all except the nasty people (who you don't want to work for anyway) will most likely either give you 30 minutes of their time or fix you up with someone to talk with. Remember that you need to make the research subject relevant to them and also you need to create a report

---

[11] http://blog.penelopetrunk.com/2013/04/23/new-paths-to-a-great-job/.

and give them some feedback. If you are really serious you could ask your local Chamber of Commerce or other local business development organization to let you talk about your research to their membership base.

Another way to do this is to approach your local Chamber of Commerce or similar organization and say you'll do something free for their members. If you are a software genius you could offer to do a complimentary software audit. You give them two or three hours. Any more and you start to charge. You can do the same with things like marketing, communications and how well they are using social media as a recruitment/publicity tool.

Whatever the initial outcomes, these sorts of efforts give you one thing above all else – visibility. If people know where you are, they can hire you. If you are hiding your light under that proverbial bushel, well it's simple – you're stuffed!

Many years ago, there was a piece of advice about the man who built a better mousetrap and the world beat a path to his door. The truth is different. You can build the biggest and best mousetrap, but if you don't tell people where to buy it they can't. Everything about business is visibility. Start with the first thing that needs to be visible – YOU.

DO THE MATH – PLEASE!

In Amrit Thind's advice, there was a piece about the network starting with those people closest to you, family and friends. Let's take this a little further, so you realize the importance of getting this right.

If you are a genius, if you graduated in the top 5 percent, fine. Otherwise you may well struggle to get work. So, look to those nearest to you. It starts with mum and dad, and then your uncles, aunts and cousins, followed by the people in your social circle or sports club. And then it is a matter of mathematics.

Think about it this way. I bet you know 50 people really well. I mean 50 people who, when they call and you pick up the phone, you recognize by voice. Indeed, I find that most people, if they sit down and make a list, usually know close to twice that many – 100 people.

So, here is how it works. Let's assume that you know 50 people, and that all those people also know 50 people. Now, some of them will know people that other people know, so let's knock off 20 percent for that. Here's what you end up with:

50 × 50 = 2,500, less 20% = 2,000 people.

Assuming I'm right and everyone knows 100 people, you end up with:

100 × 100 = 10,000, less 20% = 8,000 people.

Now, if you can't find a job with a result like that there is really no hope for you!

HOW TO WORK FOR YOURSELF – SOME THINGS WE'VE LEARNED

What's it really like to try and get a start-up off the ground? We asked some of the entrepreneurs at Birmingham Science Park, where there are over 60 small firms trying to make it through the initial start-up stages, to give us some insights. Here are some of their comments, which make interesting and educational reading.

These are real entrepreneurs (all small-time operators), talking about the real "working for yourself" issues that they face every day.

- The people skills you need are the ones you don't get in a corporation. In a company people try and stab you in the back, in your own business you have to learn to persuade people, use your time effectively.
- You need to learn to survive on five hours sleep a night.
- I love the idea of networking. But to be effective, I want to know who I should meet before I get there. So always get the guest list BEFORE you go.

- If you are going to network effectively you need to be clear what you want to get out of it, what skills you want to promote and have a reason for why people should want to talk to you.
- This is a selfish pursuit. You need to do it for yourself.
- I learned more in six months doing this than all the time I was at university.
- How did I get started? I blagged my way into a software job and learned it from there.
- When we started we were like a family. Then, as soon as we started making money it fell apart; we needed offices, people, equipment – the culture changed.
- I found myself looking forward to the weekend, looking forward to the end of the day. Then it was a can of Red Bull to get me through to lunchtime. Yessir!, it was time to leave, the magic had gone.
- For me, the fun is in the start-up phase, then I get bored.
- For the first four weeks my software developer lived in a room at my parents' house. I still live there; it's the only way I can afford to keep going.
- The hard part is splitting your talents – multitasking.
- Oh, yes, we had an organizational structure. But all the boxes had my name on them.
- You are, in fact, a prisoner to your bank balance.
- There's a little model called "the Rule of Three." It goes like this: everything takes three times longer, is three times more expensive and is three times harder.
- Where does it go wrong? You don't get the revenue generation quick enough. So the question is: how big IS the cushion you have?
- You have to be brave enough to see it isn't working and change it.
- There is a need for people who can take an idea from one to 50 people in 12 months flat. That's really the time you have.
- Businesses that start in an incubator environment have a lot more chance of success than in someone's back bedroom. Why? The peer-to-peer mentoring that you can access is priceless.

chapter 6
Educate, Educate, Educate

The complex world that we are now facing is going to bring a lot of change to one, very specific, area – education. Our need to be ever better prepared for the working worlds of the future has never been so visible.

Moreover, as previous chapters have made clear, many school and college leavers feel that they have been ill-prepared by their teachers and the overall educational establishment for obtaining the required skills for success in the future working world. It would seem that although many of the tools exist, we are not, perhaps, using them in quite the right way.

Education is a huge subject. Certainly there is room for a whole book on the next steps that education should take. So here, I am going to scratch just a few surfaces and look at the future of the business school, and then at how we will coach and mentor our colleagues and employees over the coming years. Whatever happens in the worldwide workplace in the future, they are going to be exciting and perhaps uncertain times.

The reason is that there seem to be a large number of potential conflicts that need to be resolved across the broad spectrum of business-related education.

As in other areas of the working equation, education needs to embrace technology. But exactly how and in what form are very much under discussion. For example, a digital world allows people practically anywhere to access knowledge at any time they choose. Many of the world's top universities have created free access to forums and put every lecture on line. But does that work? Most certainly you can look and listen, but can you learn? Without the expert to interpret what is being taught, aren't we in danger of re-creating another version of the old saying "A little knowledge is a dangerous thing?"

The other by-product of the digital revolution in the education sphere has been the advent of MOOCs (Massive Open Online Courses). While these have been lauded as bringing the best of a subject to vast numbers of people – who might never have had the opportunity to access this quality of information – there is also a strong backlash. Most of that, again, is tied to the thought that unless you can explain, you cannot train.

Indeed, a survey by the European Foundation for Management Development (EFMD),[1] of over 5,000 students at 37 business schools, reported that "more than 50 percent of participants 'would not study a business program in a MOOC.'" And in a parallel question to managers, over half said that "I am uncertain of what a MOOC offers and how it can be part of a business degree." They went on to add that "I would not recruit a graduate that had only studied online."

Still, with the huge demand for business-related education, there will always be the need to add the digital element into courses. Part of that is driven by the difficulty of getting student visas for those who want to study in other countries. This is particularly pressing for students from China, and other parts of Asia and Africa, who want to study in the US and Europe. To accommodate the demand, many of the business schools in Europe and the US are increasing the amount of online study so that students can stay in their own country for longer

---

[1] "See the Future – A Brave New World for Business Education," EFMD, May 2013.

and get access to face-to-face teaching for weeks rather than months. The other option is to create "real" campuses in these countries, as many of them have already done. These developments are, of course, fueling huge demand for more and more lecturers and teachers in the developing world (a massive and growing job opportunity).

But, there looks to be no end in sight to that huge demand for education in the West. Much of this is driven by the simple fact that getting a degree from a European or US university has a huge professional and social cachet for the recipient. However small and insignificant in academic terms it may be, holding an MBA or BA from a school in Geneva, London, Paris or New York goes down very well in Asia and Africa.

So will that love affair with a degree from a European business school, however obscure, continue? Patrick Faniel, president of the UBIS University in Geneva, sees a further focus on emerging markets as the way forward, particularly for all but the biggest players. "We have increasing links with emerging countries – Asia, Africa, the 'Stans,' because that is where the customers and the competition are." And he adds: "The model of the traditional business school cannot last too long (except perhaps if they only target the elite-type students). In any case that will only work in a few countries, the US, UK, France perhaps."

KEEPING THE WESTERN MODEL ALIVE

Business education as we know it today has been invented and evolved in the West – notably in the US and Europe. But is this model going to survive; are the needs and styles of emerging economies going to mean a new-look business school with a program adapted to the market it serves?

EFMD's Eric Cornuel doesn't see things changing all that much. "Asian business academics are not about to abandon the canon of Western business education," he says. "For a start, it has proven applicability and, second, most of the Asian academics were educated in it. But they are not embracing it totally." He adds to that by saying, "Many realize that it will need adapting to the reality of the Asian way of doing business – for example the role of networks, the importance of family and other relationships."

But Cornuel ends with a view that, "Intriguingly, as they do this, so there will be much from their research for Western business to learn."

UBIS University's Patrick Faniel thinks that some changes have already happened and it is in our willingness and ability to integrate new ideas that future success will be shaped. "The mistake we often make is to assume that emerging economies will first go through 'our pattern of education' to reach their future. That their path is just the same and they can use the same recipes." He adds: "I really don't think this is the case. They have already built new models. We already have many examples of the way they see business, how they manage people. It's not a question of being worse, better, adapted or ethical – it's just a different way."

He explains that "my message to my students is [to] take the best out of their country and the rest of the world and discover how to bring these things together."

The threat to European and US mastery of the MBA and its associated degrees is not lost on Eric Cornuel, Director General of the European Foundation for Management Development (EFMD), either. "Competition is not just coming from other more-or-less traditional providers such as highly professional business schools in Asia (notably China and India), but from new providers utilizing new and sophisticated internet-based teaching technology," he says. "These could change the management education business model overnight, particularly combined with a second development, the withdrawal of many governments in developing countries from their traditional role in funding higher education due to financial crises and increased austerity."

He predicts that "When you add on the fact that this coincides with a competitive global market in management education and business development, then, while it may be too much of an exaggeration to predict a 'perfect storm,' there seems likely to be some heavy weather ahead."

Some of that heavy weather is going to come from the clouds of confusion that are engulfing many business schools and colleges as they struggle to meet emerging demands. One place where the hand-wringing of what to do next is already over is on the shores of Lake Zurich, where Peter Lorange has created his future model at his eponymous school. "I am taking a client-driven perspective," says Lorange, "I am asking companies what do they want to learn, rather than asking professors what do they want to teach."

No permanent faculty

Believing that this innovative method is the way forward to deal with the complexity that companies face, Lorange continues: "Companies tell us what they need and then we find the professors to deliver. For this reason, there are no permanent faculty members at the Lorange Institute. Instead, world-class teaching and research professionals are drawn on an ad hoc basis from leading international institutions to build flexible customer-driven programs that guarantee executive participants access to the best faculty in their field."

Peter Lorange says that this is executive education's approach to that operated by the car maker Porsche, "where the company outsources much of the research it needs, knowing that it can only keep ahead of Mercedes and its other rivals by tapping into the best wherever the company can find it."

UBIS' president, Patrick Faniel, agrees with this model: "Instead of transferring knowledge, a business school has to make their clients extremely adaptable and aware of different ways of doing and thinking about business." He emphasizes that "today this is about sharing experiences – using people who have actually done it. Not professors or consultants."

There's agreement from EFMD's Cornuel too. "It is certainly true," he says, "that business schools must be increasingly flexible and adaptable. A lot of this will be due to the effects of technology, funding and globalization. And it is certainly true that most of these will require greater flexibility from faculty."

Asked if he thought that Peter Lorange's approach of having a business school with no permanent faculty, but "borrowing" what you need as and when you require it, was a model for the future, Cornuel responded, "Peter's experiment with his school in Zurich is extremely interesting and we, like many others, will follow his progress closely." He adds, "One can understand, even to some extent agree strongly with, his underlying philosophy and what he is trying to achieve. However, I am not sure that as a model it can be widely applied to the general populations of business schools."

Cornuel has a point. This buccaneering approach works well on a small scale. But could it ever be practically applied to major business schools or other academic institutions? Suffice to say that making that kind of transition would take a long time, especially if the faculty was not totally sold on the idea or had a hard time adapting to new technology.

Indeed, in that EFMD study cited earlier, over 60 percent of the participants said that, "for academics, technology often means little more than using a PowerPoint presentation." There's the concern. We already know that the academic world is fighting a rearguard action in some quarters, resisting too much change as it sees long-established norms of behavior being slowly eroded away. Furthermore, we also know that many academics and those who populate the educational establishment are rather out of touch with the real working world. So if that is all true, how do we get real learning that meets today's needs back onto some type of sensible agenda?

Geneva-based educator Alain Haut – who swapped a 30-year career in business as a senior manager for a current one in academia – also thinks that the Lorange experiment is a great idea, but may well not be scalable. "I find the Lorange concept much more flexible than the traditional B-school programs," he says, "but individual programs may lack coherence." Then Haut adds, "In reality, the just-in-time teaching concept is always difficult to pull off. Real business practitioners are not going to be easy to reserve months in advance and there is always a risk they will cancel."

Fifty-fifty anyone?

Despite how difficult it would be to make it function in practice, Haut still thinks it should be tried. "If it was up to me," he suggests, "I would insist that every business school has a better split between (former) business practitioners and academics. Fifty-fifty would seem a good idea – while my own experience shows that it is more like 85 academics to 15 practitioners. This is especially true if we count what I term the 'obsolete experience' of professors who left the business world 15 years or more ago."

Haut adds one more item to his wish list: "In addition, I would challenge the 'almost permanent tenure' of professors by creating a very critical performance appraisal process, carried out by real business people – not only by students and peer academics."

All these points that Alain Haut makes are critical issues if we are to make any headway in reforming the system and – perhaps more critically – give business the type of training and development it wants. But it also highlights that while a relatively small, specialist school can offer a program stuffed with a star cast of practicing managers – who also happen to be able to tell the story and communicate effectively with students – doing this at scale could well be a hard, if not impossible, task. Peter Lorange's concept works for him, but may prove a stretch for others. This leaves us with the situation of not being quite sure what really comes next. As Cornuel (EFMD) has predicted, there's some heavy weather on the way.

Patrick Faniel (UBIS) makes this comment: "Being really honest, the key challenge we are facing today – and this is just the beginning of it – is that no one really knows where we are going. The only thing that is certain is that we are getting there very fast!"

Faniel continues: "The time of definite plans, of feeling secure in the direction you are taking, is gone forever. We are faced with working with models that we really don't know much about and these shake up our certainties. Additionally, the speed of change is accelerating, creating situations we have never been faced with before and, as a consequence, for which we are not fully prepared."

Picking up on what Peter Lorange had to say about asking companies what they want to learn, Faniel concludes: "Management development programs must prepare managers and other professionals to be extremely open and adaptable. We need to teach them how to be much more in line with what the market needs – customer insight and customer centricity."

This view is amplified by business lecturer Alain Haut, who thinks that if we want practical people to teach the practical courses we need then we will have problems: "If we can't get real practitioners, because of the problems of getting them to commit time, we will end up with learning from consultants," he explains, "And if we do that, you have to ask the question 'did they ever work in a global business environment, at what level and how recently?'" Then Haut answers his own question by saying, "After meeting many academics/consultants, I would say that very few have the real and practical business insights!"

Asked, on the basis of that comment, whether he sees a future for the B-School, Haut replies: "Yes they will survive, but they will have to adapt and will need to renew their teaching staff regularly to get the best possible practical insights. However, I would have to add to that, why would the best business people be attracted by an academic career?"

Finally, he points out that "they will also have to coordinate a lot better with corporate training departments to create synergies between business needs and the education they provide."

More about the faculty of the future

There are many business school academics around the globe who are watching the model created by the Lorange School of Business in Zurich very closely indeed. And while some think that it is a model that can't be grown above a certain size, it is still worthwhile considering how it has been put together.

A lot of it comes down to Peter Lorange himself. He has very much projected his enthusiasm and his personality into the school. Here is how he describes the concept in his own words, from the creation of the faculty model to the day-to-day operations. Is this the way we should be thinking and adapting other schools – not just for MBA students but for others as well?

So, why is this visiting faculty so critical to the success of the model?

> A dynamic, visiting faculty brings freshness, vitality, creativity and richness of input. I know that we won't capture the creativity of our faculty members – and hence improve our offerings to customers – unless we establish a strong culture of dialog and exchange of ideas. And because I want our participants to share their experiences we also extend the meeting-place culture to them as well. So, I don't have an office. I sit in the lobby of the school at a large table. That makes me more accessible to everyone – after all they can't help but notice me as they come into the building! Most important, I am visible and accessible to our faculty and to our students. I don't have to say things like, 'my door is always open.' If I am sitting at my table everyone knows they can come and talk to me.

There probably aren't too many other deans of business schools (or any kind of school for that matter) making their "workplace" the main lobby of the building. But it does send a message that you can't help seeing and hearing.

And Lorange says that his aim is "that this openness will create alignment, team-building and creative problem-solving and help maintain a stakeholder focus."

Lorange then explains further his model of a "guest faculty." "My keen wish to eliminate silo thinking lay behind the decision to have no permanent faculty. This has the additional benefit of allowing us to draw on the best professors available to teach and deliver a particular academic program, irrespective of where they have their primary appointment." He continues: "We also try to identify two professors for each program. One typically coming from a US-based academic context and the other from a European or Asian context. This allows us to deal with the fact that most cutting-edge issues at the state-of-the-art level are dilemmas for which there are no specific answers and alternative perspectives must be considered."

Fully aware that he might be accused of poaching talent from other schools, Peter Lorange is all too familiar with the implications and has a model that clearly takes care of this sort of issue. "Two main arguments need to be raised in defence of the Lorange model," he suggests. "First, research is critical to making sure that the teaching is cutting edge and the Institute expects all faculties to do research that is directly related. Not only do we pay for this research, but we also make a contribution to the research budget of the business school the faculties are primarily attached to." He adds to that: "We make sure that all research carried out by faculty is shared in conferences and meetings to create a collegiate atmosphere and that new ideas and information get back into the classroom as soon as possible.

"Second, and what I think is the most critical fact, is that each faculty member takes back to his or her host institutions valuable innovations relating to course design, innovative classroom sessions, insights to benefit research and so on." And he concludes with the idea that "These types of innovation might normally be hard to implement for a faculty member at his or her host organization, given the resistance to change that tends to be normal. Thus the Lorange Institute might be a resource to help others innovate faster."[2]

---

[2] Some references and concepts in the discussion with Peter Lorange were based on his book *Leading in Turbulent Times*, Emerald Publishing, 2010.

A few more facts

While the jury may be out on whether Peter Lorange's vision will ultimately work, it would be remiss not to mention a couple of what I think are highly salient facts. Part of the problem with reforming and reshaping any part of academia and the education system is the well-entrenched attitudes of those in charge. Unless they can see real advantages in changing, they aren't going to. Despite what keen observers such as Alain Haut would like to see, the truth is that much of business education is taught by people who have not updated their courses for 15 or more years.

Now, the reason that Peter Lorange may have a very real chance of pulling off something unique is that, unlike almost any other business school on the planet, the Lorange Institute of Business is owned, 100 percent, by Mr Lorange himself. This makes pushing the change agenda so much easier. No discussions with recalcitrant faculty members, no assistant deans to placate, no major external donors to please. Oh no! Peter Lorange can do it his way, because there is no one to tell him he can't. There are very few people in that position anywhere.

So if I was a CEO and wanted to get the best for my top team, I know what I'd be doing. Taking the train to that lakeside business school and talking about the best way to get my people ready for tomorrow. Believe me, Peter is a good listener, but also full of brave, new ideas, and he has a better chance than almost anyone to get them implemented.

70 – 20 – 10

Of course there is a great deal more to education than getting MBAs and other business-related diplomas. But the way that pioneers such as Peter Lorange are thinking is going to be critical to the future of the formal side of business education. However, there are other aspects that need to be addressed.

The first is what's the best way to learn? With many employers saying that so many first-time job applicants don't know how to apply for a job and don't have the right skills, what's the best way to solve that?

In interviews for the book it became very clear indeed that it is with the schools and colleges that the responsibility to prepare future generations for the workplace must lie. To do that, they are going to have little choice but – rather like the academics of the business schools – to start to give up age-old habits and create programs that meet today's needs.

We know that most human resource professionals are convinced that most learning takes place on the job, but even so, many educators are still pushing classes and rote learning as solutions. Simply put, the 70 – 20 – 10 rule seems to work best. That's 70 percent experience on the job, 20 percent in mentoring by fellow workers and just 10 percent in formal classes.

More than that, there is much emphasis from many companies – who report difficulty in getting the right recruits – that what's needed is to give students an education where they learn how to learn quickly. This means that you can plug people into what's been termed "just-in-time" education. Give people basic tools and skills to learn easily and adapt and you can teach the job as and when the need arises. This is no doubt the system that many workplaces of the future will adopt.

EDUCATING TO ERADICATE POVERTY

There is, of course, another way of looking at education in the working world. Far removed from the classy business schools of Europe and the US, others are bringing not just hope, but very real change to thousands by offering micro-loans that create new vibrant societies.

Former banker and entrepreneur Jim Prouty is just one of those people. He has hung up his dark suits, sober ties and wingtips and invested his many years of experience into helping out with micro-loan projects in South America and India. Here's how he describes his experiences in a totally different part of the world-wide workplace (but these sorts of initiative are just as important in terms of making progress in the highly varied workplace of tomorrow):

> The global banking system does not want to go down market to reach the few billion of unbanked people in poverty. Banks have been hit for years trying to go down market just trying to do small business loans to very small companies. They don't even consider making loans to these two billion of desperately poor people because (they think) it's too risky and too expensive to administer.
>
> Then, in 1976, Muhammed Yunus, a Bangladeshi, identified the need to help these people living in highly remote parts of Bangladesh. He went to the tiny villages and met with the heads of households (95 percent women) most of whom were making a living and supporting their families with the profits from their microbusinesses (these are typically a one-person operation). These businesses could be simply owning a cow and selling its milk, or a woman weaving baskets or making cloth. The main thing he discovered, and this has been the case ever since, is that these women realized that if they did manage to get access to a loan from a microfinance institution (MFI) they had better pay it back. Reason? There may never be a chance again to get a proper loan at an interest rate that was not extortionate, although rates are high in this business. Because the banks really didn't want to be in this business, loans prior to this time (and this is still the case) could only be obtained from the "money lenders" who were/are loan sharks charging wildly high rates of interest.
>
> The second thing that Yunus figured out is that in small villages where everyone knows each other, with some being members of large extended families, these women (and some men but mostly women) stick together supporting each other during difficult times. This realization led to a concept started by Yunus called Group Lending/Grameen Model. This basically means that the microfinance company/lender will make individual loans to say a group of 20 women for let's say £200 to each person but that it will be the responsibility of all of the women in the group to guarantee each individual loan of all participants so that they all become equally liable. Because the need and peer pressure are so great, coupled with the fact they know they have to pay back the loan or be subjected to the loan sharks, on average 98 percent of these loans are paid back like clockwork over (typically) a 24-month

period. Microfinance companies also make what is referred to as an Individual Loan. This is typically a bit larger in size, perhaps up to £1000, but there's no group guarantee process. The loan loss rate is higher on these loans but still typically below 5 percent.

Most of the microfinance institutions (MFIs) are private and started by entrepreneurs (they're called promoters). There are also a lot of very wealthy individuals and organizations that want to do some good with their money so getting access to funding isn't all that difficult although it's become more so lately as investors have been hit by the 2007–2013 global recession. People like Bill and Melinda Gates and Michael Dell are big in this sector. The Ford Foundation has also been actively involved from the beginning. Today, private equity (PE) and pension funds wanting to do something worthwhile socially (the pension funds not the PE firms) have jumped in. In short, there's plenty of money around if you have a convincing story.

The loans typically are for as little as £100 but average £200 to £300 all around the world. The investors have done pretty well because the interest rates are still quite high (on average 30–50 percent) per annum and, as mentioned, the borrowers pay back 98 percent of what they borrow. That makes for a very good business.

The majority of MFIs only make loans and nothing else. Increasingly, however, these MFIs are offering insurance. Not surprisingly, the individual loans (not the group loans) are made predominantly to farmers who are subject to financially devastating crop failures, animal diseases/deaths etc. Insurance is now being offered to cover these losses. Insurance is also being offered to the group borrowers. The message to them is that their small business can be wiped out if there's an untimely death and funeral expenses need to be covered.

Some MFIs are also encouraging savings accounts for the same reason. Michael Dell made a large grant (almost all of what he, Gates, Ford and others like them do is to make a grant not an investment or loan) to help companies put in the technology to offer savings accounts, realizing that savings is a way to protect against unforeseen problems that will set a family back. The idea is to gradually expand these services so people are getting traditional financial services.

> Microfinance is most definitely helping millions of very poor people around the world. The majority of the assistance is, as I mentioned, just to keep them going but there will of course be many examples of a small first loan to a borrower being the start of a significantly better life where the loan allowed them to expand beyond what would have been possible without the first loan. We have made hundreds of loans for example to a seamstress who owns one old Singer sewing machine and we lent her money to buy a second, doubling her output and allowing her to employ a daughter, sister or friend.
>
> Here's a typical case. A woman and members of her family started a wonderful (vertically) integrated business making little aluminium pots used in kitchens and to store things. You see these things all around India. We made a series of five separate loans to this family located in a tiny village about 200 miles east of Hyderabad. The first loan was to the family member who bought the aluminium ingots. The second loan was to the family member who melted down the ingot. The loan we made to him was for a small third-hand furnace. The third loan was made to a group of three people who owned the molds next door into which the melted aluminium was poured. The fourth loan was made to another group that would bang out the imperfections in the molded pots and then use a type of grinder/sander to finish off the product. The fifth loan was made to the family that bought all these goods and sold them in a market about ten miles away. They were all delighted with their businesses and as a result had the nicest thatched houses in the village and were able to send their kids to school, which consisted of walking to a large tree (for shade) about two miles away, sitting under it with about 20 other children of all ages and sharing five pencils and one notepad to learn their sums.

Mentoring as a solution

You can also make sure you do another thing very well – mentoring. Having someone at your elbow encouraging you – especially when things aren't going right – is one of the best "at work" things that can happen. Mentoring is certainly a key part of on-the-job learning. But one thing that should be pointed out is that a great deal of the mentoring initiatives in organizations seem to involve a one-way street – an experienced person helping out and advising someone junior to them.

As Aaron White of the Center for Creative Leadership comments, "I think that 'seasoned' people who don't want to retire completely are huge assets. I know a lot of young people that have difficulty in navigating the path of post-college life and could benefit from learning from someone who has been through it before." He adds, "Older individuals are more in tune with themselves and are better at managing relationships – something that young people could really learn from."

Just doing that sort of mentoring is OK, but it can also be very effective when companies establish reverse mentoring programs too. The way this works is that while experienced staff can have a great impact on helping less experienced staff or new arrivals find their feet and learn the right skills, those younger people can do the same for their elders. This has be seen to be particularly effective in broadening the IT skills of older workers, by having a younger – and more up-to-speed – mentor help them embrace the possibilities of new technology.

Some words on coaching

Hanneke Frese is arguably one of the world's top coaches. Qualifying by training at schools as diverse as INSEAD and Harvard, she is a respected and influential voice in the global coaching fraternity. Much of her value to her clients has come from the fact that she was able to transition from a hugely successful corporate career (she was on the managing board of Zurich Financial Services and a senior figure at Citicorp) to an empathetic, solo role as a coach to senior managers and business leaders. The value she brings to the party is that she has really "been there and done that," so knows what leaders go through as their careers progress.

So what makes a good coach? In Hanneke Frese's view:

> It's important to understand the differences between coaching, consulting and mentoring. The International Coaching Federation

> defines coaching as *"partnering with clients in a thought-provoking and creative process that inspires them to maximize their personal and professional potential."* Consulting can be described as giving specialist advice to other professionals in an expert field. There may be consulting moments in a coaching relationship if the coach also has a professional background in the field in which the client works. A mentor, on the other hand, tends to give expert advice, information and knowledge to the client and there is a sense of the mentor having more experience than the client. Mentors can come from the same organization or industry ... But the terminology of these three different roles can be confusing as they are often used interchangeably by people less familiar with this field.

However, Frese advises that you need to make sure that you are using fully accredited, recognized professionals when you step into the coaching arena: "coaching is an unprotected professional field but more and more organizations look carefully at the qualifications the coach has and will look for professional training by such organizations as the International Coaching Federation (ICF), INSEAD (Executive Master Coaching and Consulting for Change) or the Center for Creative Leadership. These are just three well-known organizations but there are many more organizations and institutions where experienced coaches can obtain further training and development themselves, be it in clinical psychology, systemic constellations, team dynamics or a whole range of other approaches as well as accreditations in psycho-dynamic tools."

And Frese goes on to warn potential users that you really do need to know your coaches' professional background before you take them on. "Clearly a coach who lacks self-reflection and awareness can bring a lot of his or her own issues into the relationship," she warns. "This can be unhelpful to the client who should be in the center of the relationship. In such a case the coach may be tempted to use the coaching relationship for the benefit of his or her own ego rather than to hold back and allow the client all the necessary safe space to explore what behaviors may get in the way of success. Such coaches may not necessarily do damage but one can imagine that the results would certainly be sub-optimal. I can imagine that clients would disengage such coaches when they realize that the bi-personal relationship has ingredients that undermine a healthy and useful working relationship." And while not every coaching case is a complete success, Frese goes on to say that "often it is the beginning of the client leaving less useful behaviors behind and substituting those with behaviors that are more impactful in the current stage of career and context." She continued as follows:

> Recently a senior leader in a client company told me that he felt that the work I had done with one of their high potential young leaders had been extremely impactful. In fact the total cost of the coaching track added up to the cost of an executive MBA program at a leading business school, but he felt that the coaching had provided such targeted support with long-lasting benefit that he was pleased with his decision to opt for coaching. He also felt that the blind spots the client had were so severe that had the coaching not taken place it may have led to a situation of derailment. In this case the impulsive responses were indeed rooted in childhood and early adult experiences and using the clinical approach the coach was able to help the client gain a better understanding of how past situations destabilized the current context at a subconscious level.

> Now the client is performing at a high level not only from an expert and leadership point of view but also as a member of the team. Situations that used to trigger emotional reactions destabilizing relationships are now dealt with in a much more constructive manner and the client is more serene, both at work as well as at home. Pre-burnout symptoms were clear at the beginning of the coaching track and a full-blown burnout syndrome was avoided, benefiting the individual client as well as the client organization.

As Hanneke Frese points out, done effectively, coaching can not only help in personal development but bring people back to being useful and productive members of a team. This type of skillful coaching is set to continue in the workplaces of tomorrow. Just be sure you have the right coach for the tasks you are setting them and the results you want to achieve.

E-learning and d-learning (digital learning)

Finally, there's one other area of workplace education that can't be left out: e-learning. Too many of us have been subjected to the excessively boring, rote learning of electronic education products: clicking a mouse, seeing a new screen of information. For many this has been another way (usually a cheap way) of getting basic information across to large numbers of people.

Now, however, things are beginning to change. The falling costs of making much slicker teaching modules, coupled with the rising expectations of staff brought up on high-quality computer games, are heralding an explosion of new materials. This is set to increase dramatically as the costs keep falling and the gaming industry realizes that it has a whole new world to conquer. Instead of making products for the leisure hours, it will be making products for the working hours too.

This will be a burgeoning revolution. The high-quality graphics and seamless delivery that players expect from games like Grand Theft Auto, will be reproduced to teach marketing, negotiation skills, new product development and thousands of other subjects. You'll be able to access all this material 24/7 from your phone, tablet or desktop. Taking the ideas of architect and office-space pioneer Andrew Chadwick into consideration, we will be able to learn from three-dimensional holograms of the very best lecturers and teachers. And we will be able to do that whenever and wherever we want at a very cost-effective price.

Yes, learning, education, training, personal development – call it what you will – is finally about to get a new adjective attached to it – the E stands not for electronic – but Exciting!

chapter 7
The Organizational Challenges

Peter Lorange is angry. This well-seasoned academic, innovator and business leader thinks that it is high time a lot of his contemporaries woke up to the fact that the organization has changed irretrievably – and do something about it!

Norwegian-born Lorange, whose academic career began at Harvard and includes teaching at MIT's Sloan School and Wharton and then as dean of the International Institute for Management Development (IMD) in Lausanne, has spent a lifetime trying to convince business leaders to do things in different ways. Now heading up his eponymous business school (the Lorange Institute of Business) on the shores of Lake Zurich, he feels that too many senior managers have not embraced the massive changes that have already come to the workplace.

"We've got to get away from traditional thinking," he warns, "and allow for new business models. It's not about 'I know best,' but 'the customer knows best.'" And, he claims, "disciplines are coming together and it is all about teams." What he terms, "it's we, we, we, not me, me, me!" By that he means, ditch those organizational silos that overprotective executives wallow in and work together as a single, innovative unit.

Lorange's concern is that too many organizations are not moving fast enough to keep up with the changes taking place in global society – most often driven by the digital explosion. "If we are going to be effective we must be able to really understand the modern consumer and come up with innovations that they value," he says: "This is not easy." Lorange suggests that we must not only fully understand the key technologies that drive this, but be aware of "the established bureaucracy that might block innovations." The task here, he says, is to know "who are resisting innovations."

But to be successful in the new working world, "we need to have the human talents who can network and innovate with speed and without being bureaucratic." This means, according to Lorange, that human resources (HR) professionals have to be the first ones to change and adapt. "We need to get on board the relevant HR competencies," he enthuses.

The trouble is that creating a talent process to make this work is hard. And Lorange isn't the only one to observe that we need to get a whole lot better at this.

Global people provider Manpower Inc says that we are at the dawn of what they term "The Human Age."[1] And they think that, "in the Human Age, companies must align their talent strategies with their business strategies to ensure they have the right people in place to grow and succeed." They continue: "business leaders must rethink old assumptions about work models, people practices and talent sources. They can expand their internal talent pools via retraining or by reaching into pools of talent with skills adjacent to those in demand, but they should also figure out how talent mobility programs can support their business goals."

However, getting that right isn't going to be easy either. So far, many organizational observers think that we have failed to do very much. Antwerp-based Rudi Plettinx, an organizational leadership consultant, notes that "Although we've had all the processes in place time after

---

[1] "Moving People to Work: Leveraging Talent Mobility to Address the Talent Mismatch in the Human Age," Manpower Inc, 2013.

time, in truth our developmental programs have failed."[2] He adds: "HR has never, ever become a real partner of the executive team – although there are a few exceptions. As long as senior executives have been paying lip service and see these vital initiatives as just another HR process, rather than a strategic leadership strategy process, I'm afraid that effective talent management won't really be on the radar screens of our c-suite managers."

Plettinx speaks for many frustrated leadership experts when he explains how "HR failed to make this a strategic business issue with top management and so it has festered in the inner circles of an organization's HR community." He goes on to point out that "talent is not just about having the appropriate recruitment and retention strategy, it is also about an effective development strategy." And that was the part that most organizations, so far, have missed. "What we needed," argues Plettinx, "was the leadership strategy. That is the missing link between the business strategy and our talent development solutions."

The arrival of "talentism"

Manpower's idea of a Human Age echoes that of Peter Lorange, but would only be workable if companies began to heed Plettinx' warnings and bring the whole strategy together. But Manpower goes further too, demanding that there is a huge need for not just people inside organizations to come together, but for different stakeholders to bond to make it work. And that includes the clients and customers. As Manpower Inc suggests, "The dawn of the Human Age demands that the collective group of stakeholders collaborate to find new, innovative ways to operate in a world where people with the right skills are the scarce resource and 'talentism' is supplanting capitalism."

This may be a lot to swallow in one go, the idea of talentism taking over from capitalism, but Manpower hasn't finished yet. They further their case by noting: "When a third of employers globally cannot fill

---

[2] Rudi Plettinx is the former head of EMEA for the Center for Creative Leadership, the Managing Director of Management Centre Europe and a partner of the FutureWork Forum.

positions, it's imperative that stakeholders expand their view of talent sources and incorporate strategies for attracting individuals with needed skills from across international borders." And they conclude: "To win in the increasingly volatile world of work, all stakeholders must work together to find sustainable ways to unleash human potential, no matter where it comes from."

But there is little evidence that this perceived need is going to happen in reality anytime soon. And there are lots of reasons for that. It is going to be hard work – even if there is the organizational will to do it. Somewhere, there is a disconnect between a need, that to be honest few have taken on board, and our current abilities to make these complex things happen. Rudi Plettinx believes that one of the answers lies with the plain fact that "we have become great at developing individual leaders; however, we are not good at bringing that back into the organization." He adds: "We need a more holistic and inclusive approach, leadership needs to take place in the context of the environment it is in. Most of our current leadership approaches fail on this."

But if we are to prosper in this highly complex environment where all stakeholders need to be – dare we say it – manipulated, isn't this just piling up more and more pressure on those at the top?

The answer to that would seem to be a resounding "yes." And as Dave Altman and Roland Smith,[3] two senior consultants from the Center for Creative Leadership (CCL),[4] have pointed out, "globalization has enhanced the complexity of the challenges faced by leaders at every level." They add that "the economic crisis seems to be accelerating the speed with which leaders need to find solutions for these core challenges."

---

[3] Dave Altman is the vice president for Europe and Middle East Africa, and Roland Smith is the vice president for Asia Pacific, at the Center for Creative Leadership, headquartered in Greensboro, North Carolina.
[4] David Altman and Roland Smith, "The Looming Leadership Gap," *Global Focus*, June 2013, Center for Creative Leadership.

Altman and Smith report that in talking with senior leaders around the globe they rank the top four complex organizational challenges as:

- The ability to lead and influence across multiple groups and challenges.
- How to define and communicate a clear direction for the future and create organizational alignment.
- Talent management: the recruitment, compensation, development, succession, human capital restrains and downsizing.
- Business operations and organizational performance.

All this indicates that, based on Altman and Smith's research, a lot of senior business heads know of the problems, they just haven't quite stitched it all together like Manpower Inc into the "talentism replaces capitalism equation."

But, then again, there is more commonality. Where Manpower is saying that multiple stakeholders must come together, and Peter Lorange is promoting the abolition of silos and the linking up of organizations directly with their customers, Altman and Smith have their own, not dissimilar, view. They consider the idea that there are five, what they term "mission-critical boundaries" that leaders need to overcome:

- Vertical boundaries: dealing with upward relationships (for example boards of directors) and downwards (direct reports).
- Horizontal boundaries: leading across roles, functions and units.
- Stakeholder boundaries: outside the organization.
- Demographic boundaries: gender, ethnicity, nationality and culture.
- Geographic boundaries: across time zones and subgroups within geographies.

This takes us right back to the Manpower proposal that we have to open up to new people and new ways of working if we are to grow in the future.

But complexity is now the name of the game, and possibly why the loudest voices out there are advising us that we can't do it alone – even big corporations can't do it themselves. You've got to link up, you've got to partner. You've got to seek new solutions.

It's a VUCA world

The challenging global environment that Altman and Smith's research reveals has often been termed the VUCA world; a world that is volatile, uncertain, complex and ambiguous. Professor Paul Kinsinger says that the keys to leading in a VUCA-driven world will be:[5]

- The ability to create a vision and make sense of the world.
- Understanding one's own – and others' – values and plans. Knowing at all times what you want to be and where you want to go – even while staying open to multiple routes to getting there.
- Seeking clarity and sustainable relationships and solutions.
- Practicing agility, adaptability and buoyancy (able to right yourself when you capsize!).
- Developing and engaging in social networks. To recognize fully that the days of the single great leader are past. In the new world the best leaders are the ones who harness leadership from everyone.

And amidst all the complexity and ambiguity of the so-called VUCA world, as well as a raft of economic woes, it is all too easy to take your eye off the issues around the workplace and the global talent equation. And that's something we must not do, urge CCL's Dave Altman and Roland Smith. They drive home the need to keep that talent beacon shining brightly: "We believe that the fundamental issues around talent remain," they say, "and that organizations will pay a steep price in the future if they do not invest in the development of talent. While

---

[5] Paul Kinsinger is a professor of business intelligence at Thunderbird School of Global Management in Arizona.

the war for talent may be on hold, the root challenges remain front and center stage."

They add: "Economic uncertainty and unemployment are still rife throughout the world, so one could suppose that employers have the upper hand, able to choose among the hordes of people knocking on their doors. But the reality is not that simple. A prolonged period of cutbacks, reductions in human capital investment and extreme reliance on existing top performers – all in an atmosphere of uncertainty and scarcity – can easily undermine an organization's ability to attract, develop, retain and engage skilled, valuable employees."

Some think that's already happened. Just as Manpower says that we need to be a lot more capable of trawling in new waters for the talent we are going to need, so others are saying that we may have lost out quite a bit already. Swiss entrepreneur Peter Vogel, who works extensively with the younger generations in the workplace, thinks that corporations, as Altman and Smith suggest, have got some of the talent equation wrong already: "Today, highly educated top talents are less focused on a region. They search for their professional challenge in a global context these days, that's why companies must fight harder to win and keep their top talents."

And Vogel continues with a thought that may have some far-reaching consequences if he's right: "To me this is the reason why the war for talent broke out, people looked around and had a lot more choice." He adds: "The level of education is higher than ever and the war broke out because of the global context. Today, it has become a whole lot harder for a company to present itself as an attractive employer."

But it's not just about choice. There's another word out there that adds a lot of spice to the talent recipe mix – pressure. There's no doubt that in these tough economic times, there's a fine line that a firm has to walk between demotivating its talented employees and putting just too much pressure on them. Get this wrong and, come the economic upturn, those hard-pressed employees won't be hanging around for very long.

Here's Luc De Jaeger on the talent issue: "Today, my feeling is that in some industries a lot of effort has been made to become lean. This means that companies are asking more, much more, of fewer people."[6] He explains that "To achieve this, conversely, you need the very best people," and continues: "At the same time younger employees are getting into top positions very quickly as a consequence of the erroneous idea that experienced people cost more while being less productive. This is another part of getting the talent equation all wrong."

De Jaeger has some advice for chief executives and top teams struggling to make sense of today's talent equation: "I think talent management today requires very different approaches and thinking than in the past." He continues: "It's no longer about finding the young and the brilliant and training them and keeping them for a few years. Today young people are looking for other things and maybe the talents that organizations need are with older people who you can keep and motivate."

De Jaeger suggests a few actions that organizations concerned about the talent issues should consider:

- Look at talent across generations, not only amongst young people.
- Create the conditions that will motivate those talents you need. And those conditions are probably very different between the young employees and the experienced people. Be ready to work with both.
- Be prepared to let people leave and then return. They'll have learned a lot while they were elsewhere.

Certainly the global effect is taking its toll and forcing the emergence of a new model. If we are to take in a much greater mix of people into our organizations we need to be organized for this. We also need

---

[6] Luc De Jaeger is the co-founder and managing partner of Nexum, an organizational development consultancy with offices in Brussels, Paris, Luxembourg and Geneva. Luc De Jaeger is a partner of the FutureWork Forum.

to realize that this is the start of that new Human Age. Leadership consultant Rudi Plettinx certainly thinks so: "We live in a multicultural, multipolar world," he says. "This requires us to adapt and adopt. Adapt to new people entering our organizations and adopting the best that they bring with them."

And Plettinx suggests that: "The era of American or Western leadership models being the status quo is over. We need to learn from Africa, Asia, India and the rest and evolve a new era of leadership development."

The acceleration trap

It all sounds good. But the reality for the hard-pressed chief executive is probably a lot different. Buffeted around by the storms of uncertainty, he or she can be forgiven perhaps for not getting all of this right. And, just as we were asking them to take on all this volatility and ambiguity, another issue pops into the equation – the acceleration trap.

If living in a VUCA world where the boundaries are constantly shifting is the big global, macro picture, then the acceleration trap is the opposite – what individual companies face up to. It's a real trap and one that many organizations fall into. And it's all about pressure – the wrong kind.

Professor Heike Bruch of the University of St Gallen in Switzerland says it is a journey "between high performance and exhaustion."[7] And it is a syndrome that fits perfectly with the current economic times and the need of senior managers to do stuff. Heike Bruch notes: "Faced with intense market pressures, corporations often take on more than they can handle. They increase the number and speed of their activities (raise performance goals, shorten innovation cycles, create new organizational systems). For a while these succeed, but all too often the CEO tries to make this furious pace the new normal."

---

[7] Heike Bruch is professor and Director of the Institute for Leadership and Human Resources at the University of St Gallen.

Offering a warning to many of those organizations out there who are faced with making major shifts in how they organize and manage, Bruch says that the acceleration trap catches out many an unwary business. "Not only does the frenetic pace sap employee motivation," she says, "but the company's focus is scattered in various directions, which can confuse customers and threaten the brand." As a consequence, "exhaustion and resignation begin to blanket the company and the best employees defect."

As a corporate problem the acceleration trap is everywhere, especially in the "current environment of 24/7 accessibility and cost cutting." But this ability to let the organization run away with itself and possibly self-destruct can have its origins in the fact that when it comes to leadership and talent we are still making the most basic of mistakes.

Search professional Anthony McAlister, of Thorburn McAlister, a boutique executive recruiter based in London, is disparaging about the way people are chosen to lead organizations. "Real talent management is tracking internal and external prospects simultaneously," he says, "so when someone leaves you, not only do you know who you want, but have reduced the time and cost of the process." McAlister continues by suggesting that a real part of the problems organizations face is that they are lazy about the talent process, often opting for second or third best because it's just too easy to do that. "All too often an internal candidate is favored, because the organization has failed to plan. Platitudes like 'a safe pair of hands,' and 'better the devil you know,' mask the reality of 'cheaper' and 'available.'"

And McAlister goes further by stating: "Externally recruited executives are much more likely to challenge the status quo and do not suffer from corporate 'group think,' well not at the outset anyway."

What McAlister is saying is that we all get the leadership we deserve if we are too lazy to try another way. And as the world gets that little bit more complex with every year that passes, just seeking the same easy-to-fit solutions becomes even more dangerous. As I pointed out earlier, "the different kind of Bob" syndrome is very much alive and well. The idea that you scour the ends of the earth for the perfect candidate and then in the end hire a clone of the last incumbent is all too prevalent. If Lorange, Plettinx, McAlister, Vogel, Altman and Smith are right, then we are making a poor job of leadership, talent management and succession planning. And that is largely because entrenched organizations are all too happy to continue the status quo – seemingly forever.

A lot of bad ideas

London-based consultant and coach Richard Savage,[8] who has had a long and storied career at the sharp, strategic end of human resources across Europe and the US, reckons that one of the key problems is yet another way that organizations fool themselves that all is OK, when it's not. "There's an awful lot of bad ideas around," he says, "and we often miss out on what I call the 'human factors' of candidates because of that."

Savage continues: "Yes, you need development plans, but ones that are realistic and anchored in the real world." The trouble is, according to Savage, there are too many plans that are made up "because we have to go through the exercise." And he adds, "Too many development plans are just names in boxes on a sheet of paper and then tucked away in a drawer."

And Savage throws out a challenge to organizations to take a real hard look at themselves and discover what they really do. "I'd ask the CEO to go and look at the people development plans of three years ago. Then look what has happened to the names on them. I think he or she will be unpleasantly surprised by what they find!"

Richard Savage lays out more of his views on talent management in the box on page 180, where he gives some practical insights into some of the reasons why our attempts at effective talent management often go awry.

---

[8] Richard Savage is a London-based human resources advisor and a partner of the Future-Work Forum.

THE TALENT-VALUE DESTROYERS YOU MUST TACKLE

Organizational consultant and coach Richard Savage has spent his professional lifetime challenging the status quo. What he sees as wrong in many organizations is the ability to do the opposite of what's needed. Mainly he thinks that this is a failure to truly grasp the nettle and, if necessary, undergo some painful realignment of the business. Savage is worried that we are into too many processes for the sake of it, ticking too many boxes and thinking a job is done.

"I get so tired of people who hear the phrase 'talent management' and make the wrong assumption that it is a job for the human resource department," he sighs. "It's not an HR responsibility – everyone needs to own it. And please remember that it's NOT a process! If you reduce it to a process, then it is just about ticking boxes."

Savage continues: "A tick box culture is fatal and it's certainly not talent management, but too many people think that it is. You need to persuade the CEO and his direct reports to own it." And he challenges: "If you can't persuade the CEO to do that then you are not a good HR professional."

The other danger of falling into the tick box cultural model is to turn the talent process into some one- or two-week organizational event. "How many businesses gather together all the top people for a one- or two-week talent-fest and then forget about it for the rest of the year? A great many. But they feel pleased with themselves because they have done it – and it's all locked away in that drawer in the HR department!" Savage continues: "All that sort of exercise does is put names into boxes. And, simply put, that's not talent management – that's putting names in boxes!"

He adds: "What you really need is some common way to measure performance, so you can compare against a known set of competencies."

As someone who has spent a professional career seeking out practical solutions to organizational issues, Savage worries that in too many businesses there is no one saying "strategic plan and talent in the same sentence. Because if there is no one doing that, then there's no talent management program."

And he points out that the best way to kill off talent management is to roll out a huge, organization-wide initiative. "Start small and build up," he advises, "you'll quickly kill the whole thing if you try and do it with a process across the whole company as the line managers won't stand for it. They don't need yet another initiative from headquarters in their lives. They'll just view it as another misguided HR program and kill it off."

Savage also warns against bringing in some outside consulting firm to help the talent management process. "Don't go jumping into the arms of some fancy solutions provider either," he advises, "start up small and do it yourself. That way you'll see what works for you and your business." And he rings another set of alarm bells by saying that external consultants will rarely give you what you want. "Consultants will try and sell you THEIR solution, when what you actually need is YOUR solution for YOUR business." And he argues that, in terms of the solution, "every one of those is different depending on the organization's needs."

Furthermore, Savage stresses that we need to remind ourselves constantly that it is "not the program that is the outcome, it is the end results you get."

Another piece of advice that Savage has learned the hard way over his long career is "don't make the mistake of taking the 'exclusive' approach. Talent management is not just about high performers (HIPOs)." He says that if you build your talent management plans around HIPOs you'll trigger not one, but two dangerous developments: "If you just concentrate on the high performers, you'll upset the rest of the organization. On top of that the HIPOs will get a superiority complex that you can well do without."

Harking back to Peter Lorange's thoughts at the beginning of this chapter, Savage forecasts that "concentration on HIPOs encourages 'me-ism,' when what you want is 'we-ism.'"

> Savage also warns against dehumanizing the process of talent management. While he thinks that a tick box "we've done it" culture is useless, he is also scathing about the computer scanning of résumés and other new bells and whistles that are supposed to make it easy to cut the wheat from the chaff at an early stage in any recruitment process. Savage thinks that these processes often miss out on the real talent behind the résumé.

That need to know who is where in the organization is picked up by Anthony McAlister, who says that not enough firms are really aware of the 'real-life' people situation until it is too late. "If employers do not anticipate that talent will leave them, they are either being naive or stupid," he exclaims, "the problem is that although technology is reducing hiring costs it has not changed the way most people think."

McAlister says that "all too often hiring becomes necessary as a result of a failure or an unplanned event. So what organizations need is a way of improving their bench strength against those bad days." McAlister suggests that "talent management is an art, not a science. The idea is simple; it should work like shark's teeth – when one falls out another from the row behind moves into place." The only downside on that, explains McAlister, is that "this concept relies on there being enough suitable developed people ready to step in. And, of course, it is focused internally."

And that does offer yet another difficulty. For, as he points out, "I have yet to come across a talent management program that analyses external talent. Given that between one-third and one-half of all senior placements are from the outside of an organization, this is extraordinary."

As complexity increases, it would certainly seem that knowing where your next key people can be hired from – before the crisis happens, not after – should be a key part of any organization's people strategy.

But we need better and better leaders. As CCL's Dave Altman notes, "The big question is whether our collective capacity to lead in the light of the macro-level challenges we face in society is improving." He adds,

"But given the enormity of the societal changes we face, unless we raise the collective level of leadership capability and capacity, we'll face increasingly more complex and vexing challenges in the future."

Picking up on the thoughts of several other commentators here that the age of the great, lone leader is over, as complexity makes that an impossible way to manage, Altman says that he has great faith in teams as being akin to the individual. "What inspires me more than inspirational leaders are teams that are highly productive and inspiring." He adds: "Often we focus too much attention on the role of individuals and not enough attention on how groups of people can accomplish so much more than what one individual can do."

Is profiling an answer?

One person who sees teams as critical to the future success-factor of any business is Dave Richards, whose soubriquet "Dr Dave" was earned during his time as an organizational consultant in Asia after a professional start in his native Canada. With a career that spans academia and big business, Dr Dave is now a much-in-demand organizational consultant. One of the things that he recommends is the process of profiling, which he believes gives firms a much better chance of getting the right sort of people working together.

"Profiling identifies gaps and blind spots within teams consisting of similar people. This often happens," he stresses, "when leaders recruit people they like, because they are similar or 'like-minded.'" And he adds that "Profiling can help organizations understand cultural/psychological strengths and weaknesses which can be used to guide recruitment and organizational development initiatives" (see box below).

> **DOES PEOPLE PROFILING PROVIDE AN ANSWER?**
>
> Organizational consultant Dave Richards is certain that profiling can go a long way to helping organizations get a lot of their problems not just under the microscope, but solved as well.

But – there's always a "but" – you need to be very careful how you go about it.

"First," he says, "let's make sure we understand what we're talking about. Profiling is the analysis of behavior and/or answers to questions and/or data gathered using specific devices such as questionnaires designed to investigate (wide or narrow) aspects of psychology." He continues: "this includes a range of specific personality assessments, aptitude tests, intelligence tests including standardized IQ, emotional intelligence, partnering intelligence and others, motivational assessments, preference assessments, and a lot more."

And in case you are getting really interested in this idea, Dr Dave warns, "you can often find 'free online' versions of profiling tools, but in my view, you typically get what you pay for."

So what's the big deal? What can organizations get out of profiling? According to Dr Dave there is a whole string of useful outcomes that include:

- Improved performance of teams through better understanding and appreciation of individual differences.
- Greater cohesion, alignment and communications – also through improved understanding, empathy and appreciation of differences and diversity.
- Identification of gaps and blind spots within teams consisting of similar people, which often results when leaders recruit people they like, because they are similar or "like-minded."
- Greater innovation and improved strategic leadership as organizations achieve healthier levels of creative conflict, and avoid "group think" resulting from a "diversity deficiency."
- Furthermore, profiling can help organizations understand cultural/psychological strengths and weaknesses, which can be used to guide recruitment and organizational development initiatives.

All of these advantages are linked to the concerns and worries we have been raising throughout this chapter in terms of senior management's ability to recognize and tackle the key problems they face in any "real-life" method.

However, Dr Dave warns that it can be a rather hard journey to undertake. For those organizations who think they have changed, but haven't really, it would be a possibly traumatic experience to go through. As he says, "Organizations may shy away from profiling for a variety of reasons." These include the fact that:

- They don't realize the benefits that can be achieved if it's done right.
- They've maybe had the unfortunate, time-wasting and costly experience of the multitude of amateur shrinks out there peddling themselves as expert profilers, which, as the results showed, they clearly were not.
- They view profiling as an unnecessary or onerous expense, balanced against little or no appreciation of the benefits.
- Decision-makers are sometimes afraid to open Pandora's box – using profiling at all – given that it may at some point mean exposing themselves to profiling. There's often a real fear that exposure of their own psyches to the light of day may reveal their own inadequacies and flaws.

In sum, Dr Dave explains that "getting to know yourself, and the resulting journey of learning and growth, can be a very painful process!"

But he believes that if done with proper care and attention the results can be very valuable indeed and ensure that individuals know who they are and the organization does too. "Think of it like this, there are many organizations out there that may not have floundered and foundered if they'd used profiling – and more importantly, acted on the results:"

- Enron (widely regarded as one of the great corporate disaster stories) would have exposed its sick culture. But that wouldn't necessarily have saved it from the brink.

- The Staffordshire NHS disaster (a failing UK health service) could have been avoided. But only if they had understood the implications of low motivation and disempowerment, and acted to improve communication, engagement and creative conflict.

For those who want to pursue the idea of profiling as a possible solution to freeing up corporate inertia and poor group decision-making, Dr Dave offers an action-driven roadmap for doing it right. It's a tough recipe, but it just might save some top teams from their current diet of group think:

- First, fire all the amateur psychologists and get a real one, ensuring their professional credentials are matched by extensive real-world experience.
- Select the right psychometric tools, through a creative process of assessing organizational culture and strategy, identifying the key issues to be measured in bridging between the two.
- Measure, measure and remeasure. Use the results to engage individuals (one-to-ones are essential to complement the measurements) and teams in discussing and understanding the implications of the measures.
- Keep it going. Change is a marathon, not a sprint.
- To achieve sustainable change people must be engaged in strategy and in understanding the "soft stuff."
- Don't rely on consultants who, like seagulls, will fly in, squawk a lot, eat all your food, shit all over you, and fly away! (Thanks Dr Dave for being to the point here!)
- Set a series of small goals that will incrementally achieve the big changes needed, and ensure you celebrate each and every success along the way.

As Dr Dave is careful to point out, this approach to getting to know yourself, your colleagues and ultimately your organization better is probably not for everyone. First, it takes guts to kick it off, not knowing quite where it will lead. Certainly his suggestion that there are possibly many CEOs and other senior managers who would find this type of approach worrying because of what it would expose needs to be taken into consideration. But if we are to create new strengths to manage in an increasingly complex world, perhaps this offers at least one workable solution.

The customer interaction

At the beginning of this chapter, Peter Lorange of the Lorange Business School in Zurich was adamant that the way forward in this complex world we have created, and that our organizations have to make sense of, was to interact ever more closely with the customer. As he said, "networking with key customers, to innovate with and for these customers is key now!"

Lorange also pointed out that as of right now, "we must understand the key technologies, but also the established bureaucracy that might block innovation."

IBM researcher Susan Stucky has a further take on that much needed ability to link to the customer, so that the co-creation of value becomes the norm.[9] "We need to focus on the co-creation of value with clients," she says. "Take analytics, the push into Big Data. Say a client gives us access to data, we'll help the client figure out something out there that they want to understand, ensuring the privacy and security that is necessary." She continues: "I think that in a really competitive world this is the only way you become sustainable. This is the only way you get things to stick together, by focusing very carefully on that – the co-creation of value."

---

[9] Dr Susan Stucky manages service design and service research at IBM, in Almaden, California, and is a partner of the FutureWork Forum.

And as a wake-up call to every organization on the planet, Stucky predicts the following:

> The way I'm trying to think about value co-creation – is that in this world there are patterns of value-creating interaction between and among people; between and among people and their space; between and among people and their technologies; between and among people and the business processes they're supposed to be enacting. And the contrary of course. There are patterns of value-diminishing interaction. And that it would be really nice if we had ways of figuring out which is which. Because it's going to be these kinds of patterns across different phenomena. It's going to be facilities. It's going to be facilities and IT, and HR, and all of these different pieces who need to work together. Work as a service. Space as a service. I think it's happening, and it may or may not work, of course. But we could be more deliberate in trying to understand how it could work.

Now there's a challenge to pick up on.

It's down to people in the end

But the fact remains that organizations are still struggling to come up with any successful formula that seems to work for everyone all the time. However, if we are to begin to get our organizations working in the ways that Lorange, Stucky and Richards suggest, we need to do some pretty fancy footwork.

Or do we? Are there other options on the table?

Shay McConnon is a teacher, coach, mentor, motivational speaker and also a magician. He uses the latter as part of his one-man shows designed to make people think more about not only their role in an organization, but the effect they have on their co-workers. McConnon's view is that it is some of the very basics that we are still getting wrong that lie at the heart of organizational failure.[10]

---

[10] Shay McConnon is the founder of People First and the creator of the online program "An Even Better Place to Work." He is a partner of the FutureWork Forum.

"All the evidence suggests that we are not good at our relationships, in either our personal or professional lives. The greatest source of inefficiency for most organizations lies in working relationships – conflict, mistrust and lack of collaboration," he argues.

McConnon believes that it is the failure of top management to recognize these basics that is holding us back. It isn't the complexity of today's business that most worries him, but the inability of individuals and teams to work together effectively. "To minimize wastage in working relationships, we need to be talking to each other – simple as that," he explains. "We need to have the courage as individuals to invite feedback, offer feedback and problem-solve each other's needs. We can't leave this to the managers; individuals need to take charge of their own working relationships."

He believes that the way forward is that of partnership. "Work with me. Tell me how to get it right for you." And he suggests, like Richard Savage, that again, our obsession with processes gets in the way. "When processes aren't working, everyone sits up and takes notice. But when relationships aren't working they are somehow seen as interfering with work. That's ridiculous!" he growls. "Relationships are every much a part of work as processes are. They too need to be engineered, tuned and tweaked."

He ends with the advice: "Collaborative relationships don't just happen. They must be created and maintained. And they are, at the very basic level, critical to business success."

CRAZY JOB TITLES – OR NOT?

Chief Happiness Officer may sound a little far out as a job title for some of us. But it would seem to be fairly conservative when compared with others that are in current use.

Princess of Possibilities (we assume there may be a Prince too) leads the pack of the more bizarre titles, followed by Network Society Evangelist. But we confess to also having a huge respect for anyone walking around with any of the following on their business cards: Sociopreneurial Knowmad; Third Sector Pracademic; Social Media Surgeon and Amplifier; Neworkista; Positive Disruptor; Motivational Questioner; and Maid of Fail.

There has to be an assumption that the Maid of Fail hangs out with the Princess of Possibilities.

Could happiness at work be the answer?

Assuming Shay McConnon is right and it is the interaction and wellbeing of individuals that is at the heart of organizational success and growth, then there may also be something in a movement that has gained considerable ground in the past few years – the Happiness at Work movement.

Spreading her own brand of happiness is Laurence VanHée, former Chief Happiness Officer of the Belgian Ministry of Social Security and Human Resources Manager of the Year 2012.[11] VanHée has been in the vanguard of promoting the Happiness at Work concept, which has gained the attention of a broad range of public and private firms across Europe.

VanHée explains her philosophy: "Managing people is much broader than pay and administration. From individual development to performance management, from building values to monitoring KPIs [key performance indicators], from communicating on social media to building trust in my relationships with union reps, the scope of the HR job is everything but a spreadsheet monkey's one. This is why I'm not Director of Administrative Affairs."

She continues:

> We are people – not resources. We all like to be treated as a person and this is absolutely legitimate. We are people with thoughts,

---

[11] Laurence VanHée is now an independent consultant.

feelings and talents. We are a team. We are not a human capital. We are not, together, the sum of each individual human resource. We can't, as a person or as a group of people, be considered like a capital that has to deliver a double digit return every quarter. This is why I'm not Human Capital Director. Happier people perform better. They are healthier. They are less stressed. They are more creative. They dare more. They connect to more people. They enjoy being considered as people and behave with respect towards each other. They spread their happiness around them. They shine.

And picking up from Shay McConnon's ideas, she says: "This means giving freedom to people, considering them as adults, allowing people to work in teams, asking people and the team to be accountable for their choices, trusting people. Being a boss means behaving like a resource to the team, to provide guidance, to give support, to listen and help. Putting the team first. Being egoless.

"All these small, easy steps improve the performance and the profitability of the organization. And make for happier colleagues.

"Freedom + Responsibility = Happiness + Performance.

"This is why I'm Chief Happiness Officer."

VanHée says that her working philosophy is based on five criteria:

- Don't manage. Love.
- Don't work. Have fun.
- Don't think. Think green.
- Don't complain. Innovate.
- Don't motivate. Trust.

And she is not only enthusiastic, but a true evangelist that this is the way forward and being picked up as a mainstream way of setting up a business model. Whether that is true or not, it would seem that many a frustrated CEO is prepared to give it a try. Maybe it heralds a more open working world, where employees are not afraid to air their feelings and believe they are encouraged to be themselves in the workplace. Wherever that workplace may be.

Indeed, VanHée is quick to point out that surveys show that happy people are between 10 and 30 percent more productive. They are 2x less sick and 6x less absent. According to the polling organization Gallup, companies investing in their workers' happiness have a growth of earning by share 3.9 times greater than organizations that don't. Gallup estimates that the cost of disengagement reaches $350 million a year in US companies.

Having said that, there are plenty of detractors for these kinds of approaches, who say that the modern organization is just too complex for basic ideas such as Shay McConnon's "An Even Better Place to Work," or Laurence VanHée's "Happiness" movement to really make a difference. Time no doubt will tell.

Let's hope we've moved on from the bad old days when people had to make excuses for not being at work. Even the great and good had to resort to subterfuge to get a few precious hours away from the corporate coal face. Former Chrysler chairman Lee Iacocca has admitted that "people used to ask me, 'How could somebody as busy as you go to all those swim meets and recitals, when your kids were growing up?' Well, I just put them down on my calendar as if I was seeing a supplier or a dealer that day."

And Sheryl Sandberg, the COO of Facebook, says that after her first child was born (she was still at Google) she "went to great lengths to hide my new schedule from most people. Camille, my ingenious executive assistant, came up with the idea of holding my first and last meetings of the day in other buildings to make it less transparent when I was actually arriving or departing. When I did leave directly from my office, I would pause in the lobby and find a colleague-free moment to bolt to my car."

Perhaps this is more of the perceived reality of the masses who head for the office every day and make up the workforce of tomorrow.

How to please the NEXT generation

So, as we seek out new workplaces and new workplace practices, how are corporations tackling the issue of engaging the next generations?

PeopleXpert founder Matthias Moelleney in Zurich says that "first of all they need to focus on their reputation and be seen as good employers." He continues, "If we look at how these people define work–life balance we find that the most important aspect for them is the collaboration culture at work."

Brussels-based corporate coach and teacher, Sunita Malhotra, agrees and says that corporations really need to change their ideas and recruitment practices, otherwise they'll lose out. "Generation X and Y don't want to work with the big corporations because these people are not flexible in the way they want people to work," she says. "They want to be flexible in how, where and when they work and a lot of corporates have not caught up with that yet." She continues, "They don't want the traditional nine to five ways of doing things – that was the life of their parents."

And Malhotra concludes: "Fun is a word I hear a lot."

Atanaska Varbanova of the Think Young think tank in Brussels adds to that: "Big corporations will always need bright and talented young people. However, how they manage and motivate them is something that perhaps needs a new focus. Young people today are not attracted by a world where the personal perspective is always overshadowed by corporate rules and culture."

As a graduate job seeker, Amrit Thind felt that much of what he really had to offer was ignored by those in charge of the recruitment process. He has this advice to offer:

> I often felt there was not enough communication between myself and the people reviewing my application. Rejection emails provided no feedback and this was problematic – especially if you were confident your application had been executed well and passionately ... the

> process from start to finish is drawn out and tedious, too email heavy and marked by a clear disconnect between applicant and employer. I never understood why Skype interviews were not implemented earlier on in the process and then followed up with face-to-face meetings if necessary. The face-to-face time should serve the purpose of unveiling your personality, identifying how you would fit in with the company culture and whether your vision and values align. This is probably the most important part of any application process because many of the other skills required can be learnt on the job. Organizations can make life much easier for themselves and their applicants by encouraging virtual face-to-face time early on in the process. The systems and methods used by organizations to recruit need to change. Many organizations are not thinking about the way the new economy is changing in the context of emerging technologies and social media. Jobs are still defined in narrow, functional roles, instead of roles that consist of a more open architecture. It is time to move on from the age of email and standardized online applications to an era of personalized, cost-efficient and less time-consuming interactive virtual processes. Organizations don't give enough time to get to know potential candidates beyond their technical abilities and what they studied at university.

So, corporate recruiters don't seem to shine when it comes to engaging that NEXT generation. And that same disconnect seems to color another area, dealing with entrepreneurs.

If we agree that many of the NEXT generation want to start their own businesses and be their own bosses, then to access the talent that large, medium and small corporations will require necessitates dealing with entrepreneurs. But do corporations know how to do that?

Soshi Games' founder Cliff Dennett thinks not: "I don't think most people in corporations have the faintest idea what it's like to run your own business. If they did, they wouldn't make false promises, tell you they are going to invest, then don't; drag you down to London for meetings when they know they're not really interested; force you to constantly chase them and play telephone tag. They have no appreciation for the repercussions of this on investment, marketing partners and so on."

Other entrepreneurs concur. But there's more than that to consider. Companies are going to have to quickly find other new ways of working too. All these talented entrepreneurs that the mainstream firms will definitely need to work with, in one way or another, pose one more headache. How do you work with an entrepreneur when he or she is also working for your biggest competitor? That's the new world of work, and CEOs and the rest need to get used to it. If people such as Peter Lorange and Susan Stucky are right, we not only have to work with our clients and customers, we also have to find ways to collaborate with those who, just a few years ago, we wouldn't even have considered talking to, let alone collaborating with.

A list for action

The implications for how businesses organize themselves to engage and motivate employees in the workplace of tomorrow are huge. And it would seem it can be tackled in a variety of ways. Truth to tell it will probably have to be. These complex structures that we are now having to manage (and they don't have to be giant employers these days, either) are going to need a lot of very careful management and leadership.

Many, it would seem, think that a lot of today's leaders need to go further, try new ideas, engage better with the people inside and outside the organizations. Whether we can do that or not will certainly decide who succeeds and who fails in the worldwide workplace of tomorrow.

chapter 8

The Workplace of the Future, or More of the Same?

Almost two decades ago, I wrote my first full-length book.[1] It explored how we would equip ourselves to meet the management and organizational challenges of the 21st century. In the final part of that book there were some thoughts on the next steps we may be taking, which I think are worthwhile repeating here all those years later, because I want to stress that the future of work is about people. We can have all the technology and all the great ideas in the world, but unless we have people who know how to make it all come together in a productive way it counts for very little. In embracing tomorrow, maybe this is what we should make sure of:

> Looking at most corporations – even those with an enviable track record of innovation – change, and the need for change, has always been tempered with the need for stability as well. A closer look at those successful businesses also reveals that most change (particularly the major pieces of reorganization and rejuvenation) are done in short, highly focused spurts, followed by a period of stability.
>
> It is important for all of us to keep in mind that there is a danger of confusing innovation with change. They are not – and will never be –

---

[1] *Managing in the Next Millennium*, Butterworth-Heinemann, 1995.

the same thing. Innovation is a constant process that provides us with new products, processes and services – it is vital to our future. Change is something that shakes the organizational tree, perhaps even sends a shockwave or two through the foundations. That is something that is necessary from time to time, but none of us need constant seismic shocks. Stability, knowing where the organization is going and why is equally important – indeed that sort of atmosphere actively encourages innovation.

I think these two paragraphs are important to heed. Because, although many things have happened since I wrote them in 1995, the key points still ring true. While the world may have been speeding up a few more revolutions and the executive lunch has given way to the sandwich at the desk for many, there is still a craving for stability too. In hard times like these, maybe even more so. When people – and this book is all about people and their workplaces – are in a stable environment they feel safe and secure. They are then able to do their best, because the conditions exist for them to do that. A lot of what we have unearthed in this book seems to be based on constant change. That change for change's sake. Macho managers create macho organizations where many of the employees are hurtling toward some distant, never quite visualized destination. The trouble is, it is so far away that no one ever gets there. This is not the kind of climate to foster innovation and trust.

Two decades ago, the world was a lot less global. Cell phones were a new, costly and rare phenomenon. It is strange to think that many of the great brands of today (e.g. Google, Amazon, BlackBerry, Nokia, Apple) were either second-tier organizations or did not yet exist. A lot has happened since then and a lot is going to happen in the coming 20 years too.

A dangerous game to play

Predicting the future is a dangerous game to play. We can all sit back, close our eyes and imagine flying cars (whatever happened to them?), vacations on the moon and teleportation. But none of that makes much difference to the workplace (except for the people employed to tidy up the moon after the tourists have gone home).

In another way, we can also imagine a world without poverty and hunger, with universal healthcare for all as well as clean water. That has been the wish of many for a lot more than two decades and it hasn't happened either. Without getting at all political, all you need to do is look at a globe of the earth and you quickly realize that there is a lot of it that isn't anything like as safe as it used to be. Wars and other political conflicts make much of our planet inaccessible. So we may be global in our thinking, but we have effectively put up fences around a lot of the parts we don't wish to see.

So, no predictions of flying cars and throw-away paper clothing here, I'm afraid. What I am going to do is recap on a few of the key points about the worldwide workplace and how we can take advantage of it. In doing that, I'm going to get several of my wonderful contributors, who have really helped to shape this book, to add a few of their own thoughts.

The workplace of tomorrow

Let's be honest: we see a lot of cool workplaces. They are featured in TV programs and magazines. We "ooh" and "aah" and think how that would be a great place to work. Then most of us go back to our little box, cubicle or open-plan desk, draughty warehouse or messy crew room. In truth, few of us live in the best of the 1990s' workspace, never mind that of the 21st century. Will that change? In some places, yes it will. Smart companies know that creating an attractive workspace helps to attract and retain people. It also makes them more productive while they are at work.

But we also know that the workspaces of tomorrow aren't just in an office or factory – they are everywhere. And the future isn't about people working in an office or working at home or on a client's site. It's about all of those mixed and melded together. We talk of "portfolio careers" where people have 14 or 15 jobs in their working career. What we need to talk about is the "portfolio job." As we revealed earlier, people don't just work at home five or six days a week. Most have a mix. Two days at home, two at an office location, one with a client, or another permutation based on this. This is the new workplace – everywhere at any time. And technology – particularly the digital revolution that shows no signs of stopping – is the enabler of much of that. It is, in fact, pointless to try to predict the next technological breakthrough. What we need to do is make sure that people have the right training to use the new technologies in the most effective way as they appear and come into mainstream use.

Technology is going to give us unprecedented access to not just new markets, but to linking up with talent we could never have ever met before. And this – probably for the first time – is not something that only big firms with access to big-buck budgets can do. Think of it this way. Communications technology today is virtually ubiquitous. It is also something else – cheap. This means that even if I am a one- or two-person operation in London, I can partner with, source from, sell to anyone around the globe. We can already see examples of this in online marketplaces. People are importing goods, having designs created and offering services that come from the other side of the world. The future that pundits keep writing about is already here.

An office where?

Back in 1982, just over 30 years ago, a young architect and office planner, Andrew Chadwick, entered a global competition organized by the Dutch electronics firm Philips. The brief was simple, if ambitious. Design the office of the future. What Chadwick and his team concocted was a true thinking-out-of-the-box scenario. In fact it was the opposite of that, thinking in-the-box! Because what they came up with was the "Office in a Briefcase" concept. They installed a tape recorder and a keyboard inside a briefcase. When the lid was opened, the recorder switched on and a voice intoned, "I am the office of the future. The office as we know it will diversify from its present fixed location into a multiplicity of places. The office, your office, is where you take me ... "

Chadwick and his team won the competition outright. It was an interesting – and practically accurate – prediction of the future. The only things missing were weight, size and connectivity. Few then could see that by 2013 you could have in your pocket a device that gave you access to the world's knowledge and to reach and see anyone anywhere if you had their magic number.

> **SEVEN BILLION AND COUNTING**
>
> According to software firm Cisco, by the end of 2013 there were over seven billion internet-enabled mobile devices on the planet. It is set to match the world's population sometime in 2014.

So, we'll let technology take its course and just learn to use it for what it can do for us.

But, as we are essentially talking about people and work, think of it another way too. My colleague Cliff Dennett, the founder of Soshi Games in Birmingham, UK, thinks that many organizations are still missing a trick when it comes to sourcing talented people. He knows we have the technology. What concerns him is that we haven't used it properly. And he delves into the online gaming world, to produce the example given below – something that should be heeded by every CEO wherever they are. Don't complain that you can't find talent – try this out for size!

Dennett explains that there's a critical feature in Massively Multi-player Online Role-Player Games (MMORPG): the "ability of people from all social backgrounds, religions and cultures to come together, online, for the purpose of achieving a task." As he points out wryly: "usually to fight a dragon or some ogre!" But the key to all this, points out Dennett, "is that these are people who have never met each other face to face (and probably never will) all uniting together to achieve a common goal."

As Dennett stresses, "Now, isn't that what today's corporations want to do? Don't they want to be able to unite their employees around the globe to achieve some common purpose?"

He's right. What these MMORPG players have done is taken available technology and used it for a common purpose – it even transcends language barriers in many cases. Now imagine if you can find the formula – probably something to do with fun – to take the energy, innovation and talent of a group like that and harness it to a corporate strategy. It can be done; it just takes someone to think it through. They may well be under the age of 20, but they'll know how to do it. Why? Because the leaders of these online games have to think strategy, have to know how to negotiate and motivate, have to be leaders of people that they can only imagine through a screen. Why can't business have some of that?

You can. Here's the advice. Go online right now. Get to a major MMORPG site – World of Warcraft will do for a start. Find a commander of a large army or other group. Make him an offer and hire him. The reason for doing this is that even if he is 16 years old he probably knows more about creating strategy and getting people to do stuff than most of your senior managers. He or she can move people, win battles, create and innovate, all the while employing hundreds or possibly thousands of people. Wouldn't you like someone like that on your side to beat up your kind of dragons – the competition?

Connectivity rules

It's that digital link that has made it possible. But it has also done something else; it has begun to change not only how we operate, but also how we think of things. While I may not be able to meet physically with some of the people I do business with, I can meet with them virtually. We can use cheap or zero-cost links and see each other. We can plot and plan, in twos and threes and even big groups. The world really is our oyster.

Add to this the innovation of voice commands and the ability to "talk" through a letter or a document, and even more the arrival of instant – and accurate – translation or interpretation in real time, and there is finally nowhere on the planet that you can't access. And if we are feeling lonely and cut-off, surrounded by nothing but a digital world, we can always conjure up one of architect Andrew Chadwick's holograms to have a discussion or an argument with! The digital revolution makes it possible to do what was unthinkable even ten years ago.

As San Francisco-based Jim Ware of The Future of Work ... unlimited says, "I do have some faith in the wisdom of the crowd. And I do believe that in today's economy and technology-dependent world, individuals have more knowledge, more information and more connections with each other than ever before in history."

This is absolutely correct. There is no reason why we can't find talent for our workplaces, we just haven't used the tools that already exist in the right way or freed our imaginations to think about opportunities in new ways. We've been too busy pushing change to think about what makes it all work – innovation.

The jobs of tomorrow

Sadly, we have also seen throughout this book considerable evidence that the education establishment – almost everywhere – is not preparing us for the brave new worlds of work that are out there. As Telework pioneer Tom Harnish points out, "The challenge today is meeting the rapid pace of change. We have schools today training people to do jobs that won't exist by the time those students graduate." Harnish thinks that "companies will have to create schools of their own to train and educate people so they have the skills and knowledge required. Something that is already happening in areas like aerospace and entertainment."

Oh yes, it is already happening on small and large scales. I have had a personal experience of this. The small IT company that keeps my business operational is owned by two brothers. They've been working together for 15 years. They're good at what they do, partly because they are intuitive and patient (solving IT issues takes infinite patience), but also because they learn on the job. Every week poses new challenges – a new virus to cure, a new product and new piece of software to master. But, through working with their clients and solving problems as they arise they stay ahead. But the issue is that they can't hire people from college, because IT graduates are too out of date to be useful. They train on old equipment, using old software, and are taught by people who are not up to speed.

That's real life. It's not about getting a certificate; it's about making an impact. Too many school leavers are ill-equipped to do that. There is a definite need to do something about this, although it is beyond me to think how it can be fully achieved. Certainly government isn't doing it and neither is the entrenched educational lobby.

Leadership – the next phase

In trying to make sense of our world there seems to be an endless pressure on leaders. But again, it would seem that for purely practical reasons if nothing else, there is no room anymore for the single, charismatic man or woman at the top. Most organizations – and they don't have to be that big – need more than one wise head to run them. So the future workplace looks like being run by highly effective teams who really know how to plan and implement strategies that keep their ship on course. This, of course, is fine if you have the right kind of leader to make sure all these people work together as a team or a collegiate group. The reality is that it rarely happens. Certainly those who peddle leadership development consulting and courses can breathe easy. There's still a lot of money to be made helping lost leaders find their way again.

We've predicted some rough seas ahead and there's no reason to think that this won't be an accurate forecast. Of course, there will be many dinosaur organizations that still worship the cult of the leader. There will be political ploys and leaders desperate to leave their legacy on an organization – possibly to its long-term detriment. All I know is that this book's research has made it clear that the VUCA world we're now in is a most unforgiving place. Volatility, uncertainty, complexity and ambiguity look set to be the ingredients for the workplace of the future. How that gets managed is the question that senior managers need to ask. And they need to get some answers very quickly indeed.

The truth is that some will and some won't. The last decade has been one strewn with examples of organizational failure brought about by ill-chosen strategies and corporate hubris. Indeed, the names of some great firms are now just a memory. This type of pattern looks set to continue. And that's why where I began is the place to end.

This was a journey to see what the global world-of-work is really like. Some of it offers real optimism, other bits are – as might be expected – a bit tarnished and in need of a good, caring polish. My personal view is that right now we have unprecedented access to the techniques and tools to create great workplaces and workspaces wherever they are. What we must not forget – ever – is that it is people who make a workplace not the other way around. I hope that you find your ideal workplace soon. I bet it won't be where you are now.

Index

"25 Best Places to Work Around the World" 104–6

acceleration trap, issue of 177–9
ActionAid 52–3
ageing workforce
   GrayHairPR 69–70
   planning for 70–1
   in public relations industry 69–70
aid sector, as a viable career 62–3
Altman, Dave 172–5, 179, 182–3
Amnesty International 53
Amsterdam 41, 75, 77
apprenticeship system 13, 43, 49, 51, 62
Arab Spring 73–4
Arumugam, Stanley 52–3
attrition rates 68
Autor, David 15
Aziz, Khalid 134–5

Bentham, Adam 33, 35–6, 39, 127–8
Best People Practices (2012) 108
Best Small Workplace (2012) 106–7
best-paid job 60
Black Economic Empowerment Act 42
blue-chip multinationals 111
body language 92, 136–9
brain drain 8, 10
brainstorming technologies 88

Bruch, Heike 177–8
Brynjolfsson, Erik 15
business education *see* education, business-related
business transactions 117

capitalism 171, 173
career scenario
   advice on looking good 118–19
   in big corporations 111–14
   career guidance 21–3
   career opportunity 20, 121–3
   choice of career 114
   for employers 117–18
   in information technology sector 114–15
   internet, use of 115–16
   job search 115–17
   portfolio career 114, 116
   social media advice 119–20
Caritas 18
Center for Creative Leadership, North Carolina 121, 123, 165–6, 172
Chadwick, Andrew 84, 89–90, 94, 99–100, 103, 168, 199–200, 202
China
   entrepreneurs in 55
   status of a job in 56
   work opportunities in 53–6

Index

climate disasters, population affected by 19
coaching 165–8
collaborative relationships 189
collective "hive mind," notion of 88–9
communication skills 92, 125
communication technology 89, 199
compensation 19, 173
competing for job 35–7
computer, as recruiter 68–9
computer crime 16
computer games 66–7, 68, 168
computer technology 15
Corliss, Richard 81
Cornuel, Eric 152–6
countries, preferred for overseas job 11–12
creative business 99
Crossley, Charlotte 96–7
crowd-sourcing
   basic tenets of 98–9
   power of 88
customer interaction 187–9
CVs, for job hunting 128–9, 135, 137, 140–1

decision-making 25–6, 94, 186
De Jaeger, Luc 176
Dennett, Cliff 45, 120, 128–30, 132–3, 142, 144, 194, 200
dependent groups 5
Dickens, Charles 14, 77, 91
"different kind of Bob" syndrome 14, 179
digital links 86, 201
digital recruitment 119
digital revolution 29, 34–5, 46, 93, 121, 151, 199, 202
digital technology
   for automation of business processes 27

   in business-related education 151
   and digital workspace 27–8
   d-learning (digital learning) 168
   future of work 90–2
   and human need for strongpoints 99–100
   project management 26–7
   in social aspects of working 28–9
distributed team, rise of 89–90, 92
d-learning (digital learning) 168
"do not disturb," idea of 100
Douglas, Hazel 63
drug smuggling 17

economic crisis 172
economic migration 8
   and benefits to country of origin 10
   countries preferred for 11–12
   immigration issue 10
   in search of better job 9
   shortage of workers 9–10
   visa issues and 10–11
education, business-related 150
   70 – 20 – 10 rule 160–1
   B-school programs 156
   coaching 165–8
   customer-driven programs 154
   demand for 151–2
   digital revolution in 151
   e-learning and d-learning (digital learning) 168
   to eradicate poverty 161–4
   face-to-face teaching, access to 152
   faculties for 154–9
   funding for 153
   global market for 154
   internet-based teaching technology 153
   Lorange's vision of 154–9

Index

management development programs 157
Massive Open Online Courses (MOOCs) 151
MBAs and business-related diplomas 160
mentoring initiatives, in organizations 164–5
performance appraisal process, for professors 156
research budget of 159
salient facts on 160
Western model for 112, 152–3
educational institutions
career guidance 21–3
impact on hiring needs 20–1
NEXT generation, effect on 20–1
eight cities, tale of 76–7
e-learning 168
Emmens, Ben 62–3, 114
entrepreneurism, concept of 39–40, 42
entrepreneurs 44–6, 97
ability to start up micro-businesses 46–8
in China 55
"Entrepreneurs for the Future" incubation program 96
impression, making 133–5
most valuable trait for 130–1
optimism for business opportunities 131–2
persuasion, power of 132–3
"working for yourself" issues 148–9
European Aid Volunteer Program 44
European Foundation for Management Development (EFMD) 151–3, 155–6
European Social Fund 43
European workforce 5
expatriates 71–2, 77

Fancello, Christina 110–11
Faniel, Patrick 133, 152–4, 156–7
Ford Foundation 163
Fortune 500 companies 98, 135–6
freelancers 97, 114, 116
Frese, Hanneke 165–7
future of work 90–2, 196
FutureWork Forum 21, 37

Generation Europe Foundation (GEF) 21, 37, 110–11
Geneva 77, 133, 152, 155
global banking system 162
global communication revolution 37
Grant, Alexis 116
GrayHairPR 69
Group Lending/Grameen Model, concept of 162

Hamid, Labeed 72–5
Hamid, Sami 54–5
Happiness at Work movement 190–2
Harnish, Tom 88–90, 92, 202
Haut, Alain 112–14, 155–7, 160
high performers (HIPOs) 181
"hire and fire" culture 41
holograms 89, 94, 168, 202
home-working 85, 90, 97, 102, 109, 128
Hong Kong 54, 71, 75, 77, 84, 135
Houdmont, Arnaud 35
Hultin, Göran 13, 31–2, 38, 53
human need, for strongpoints 99–100
human trafficking 17
Huskisson, Susan 135–41
hysteresis, in the job market 64–6

idea generation, creative 94
impression, making an 133–5
India, without aircon 103–4

industrial revolution 84
information highways, notion of 88
innovation hubs
   as model for the future 100–3
   for offering creative services 99
   rise of 97, 98
   through collaboration 98
innovators 107–9
INSEAD (Executive Master Coaching and Consulting for Change) 165–6
international aid and development sector 18–20, 62
International Coaching Federation (ICF) 165–6
International Conference on Population and Development (ICPD) 9–10
International Labour Organization (ILO) 13
internet 18, 82, 88, 115–16, 144, 153, 200
interview, job see job interview

job environment 86
job interview
   body language during 137–9
   and CV that sells 140–1
   dressing up for 137
   first impression 136
   for getting the job 136–8
   presentation for 136
   social media, use of 139–40
   technology, use of 138–9
   verbal and nonverbal skills 138
   vocal quality during 138–9
job market 5, 22, 36, 38–9
   hysteresis in 64–6
job opportunity 152
job search 115–17, 119, 122, 125, 141
job seekers 31–2, 65, 110;
   see also landing a job
   advice for 120–1, 124–6

CVs 128–9
   entrepreneurial route 130
   getting hired, prospects of 135–41
   scope for improvement 127–8
   social media, use of 120
job skills 59–60, 64
job-getting tips 119
job-hopping 30, 33
job-hunting see job search
jobs employers, global top ten 12–13
jobs in demand 60–1
   and tough to fill 61–2
jobs, of tomorrow 202–3
Johnson, Malcolm 50, 71–2

Kelan, Elisabeth 49–50
Knott, Dan 103

labor-force growth, in USA 5
landing a job
   checklist for 141
   job interview for 136–8
   prospects of 135–41
   required skills and experience for 142
   social network, use of 147–8
   ten ways for 141–7
   and "working for yourself" issues 148–9
language barriers 201
leadership skills 112–13, 178, 203–4
least-favored job 61
life skills 21, 40
Lister, Kate 88–90, 92
loans, business 162
lobbying profession, rise of 80–1
London 77
Lorange Institute of Business 160, 169
Lorange, Peter 154–9, 169–71, 181, 187, 195
Los Angeles 76, 84

McAfee, Andrew 15
McAlister, Anthony 39, 112–14, 178–9, 182
McConnon, Shay 188–92
McLean, Sandy 115, 117, 126–7
mafia 16–17
  Russian Transnational Organized Crime (TNOC) 16–17
Maier, Jens 130–3
Malhotra, Sunita 131, 193
management career 112
Manpower Inc. 13, 59, 170, 171, 173
Massive Open Online Courses (MOOCs) 151
Massively Multiplayer Online Role-Player Games (MMORPG) 200–1
Medellín city, Colombia 78–9
micro-businesses 46, 162
microfinance 162–4
microfinance institution (MFI) 162–3
Middle East workplace 72–5
migration, issue of 8–9
Mölleney, Matthias 31, 62
Morse, Teri 68–9
"most powerful" generation 23–5

New York 42–3, 71, 75, 77, 79, 81, 83–4, 107, 115, 122, 127, 152
NextSpace 97–8
non-governmental organization (NGO) 63

old-age population, rise in 5
online education 74
organizational challenges
  acceleration trap 177–9
  bad ideas, issue of 179–83
  collaborative relationships 189
  Happiness at Work movement 190–2

list for action 195
people profiling, process of 183–7
  in pleasing NEXT generation 193–5
talent management 173, 178–82
talentism, idea of 171–4
VUCA-driven world 174–7
Western leadership models 177
organized crime, global operations of
  computer crime 16
  electronic and financial crime 16
  entrepreneurism and 42
  "iceberg employer" category 16
  Russian Transnational Organized Crime (TNOC) 16–17
  white collar crimes 17
Orwellian scenario (1984) 93
overseas jobs
  countries preferred for 11–12
  money earned from 10
  reverse brain drain 10
  visa program for 10–11
Oxfam 18

Palieri, Chiara 23, 40, 120–1
people profiling, process of 183–7
performance appraisal 156
persuasion, power of 132–3
Plettinx, Rudi 170–2, 177, 179
portfolio career 114, 116, 198
problem-solving skills 15, 83, 158, 189
project management 92
Prouty, Jim 161

Red Cross 18, 44
  Code of Conduct 63
remote teams see distributed team, rise of
retirement ages 5, 56
Richards, Dave 183–6, 188

Index

robotics
 application in industrial sector 15–16
 engineering jobs, affect on 15
Routledge, Helen 66–7, 79
Russian Transnational Organized Crime (TNOC) 16–17
 "iceberg employer" mode 17

salaries and fringe benefits 18
Salpeter, Miriam 118–19
San Francisco 42, 76, 87, 202
Savage, Richard 179–82, 189
Save the Children 18, 19, 63
skills shortages 31, 58, 60, 64
small and medium-sized enterprise (SME) 7, 42, 112–13
Smith, Roland 172–5, 179
social media 116–17
 for job seeking 120, 139–40, 144
 power of 88
 rise of 82
social networks 26, 35, 116–18, 120, 133, 147–8, 174
social reputation 117
Souktel 77–8
Stucky, Susan 26–9, 85, 87, 187–8, 195

talent development 112, 171
talent management 115, 171, 173, 176, 178–82
talent search 13–15
talent shortages see skills shortages
talentism, idea of 171–4
tax incentives 41
telemarketer 61
Thind, Amrit 141, 146–7, 193
Totem Learning 66–7, 79
trades and professions, in demand see jobs in demand

unemployment 13, 24, 38, 42, 44, 46, 51, 58, 61, 64, 73–4, 96, 144, 175
unique selling proposition (USP) 78
United Nations (UN) 18
US Bureau of Statistics 59
US Patent and Trademark Office (PTO) 102–3

VanHée, Laurence 190–2
Van Massenhove, Frank 101
Varbanova, Atanaska 39–40, 121, 193
video conferencing, high-definition 85, 88
video web conferences 139
virtual communities 88
virtual walls, concept of 85–8
visa program
 quota system 11
 to recruit foreign workers 10–11
vocational education 43
vocational qualification 22
vocational skills, in demand 12–13, 39
Vogel, Peter 130, 133, 175, 179

Ware, Jim 87–8, 90, 93–4, 202
Watson, Carmen 31–2, 37
White, Aaron 121–5, 165
white collar crimes 17
wirearchy, concept of 25–6
women's employment 124
work opportunities
 in China 53–6
 competing for 35–7
 crane analogy 48–9
 "crowded out and bumped down" syndrome 33–4, 36
 digital revolution, impact of 34–5
 entrepreneurism 39–40
 European Aid Volunteer Program 44

"hire and fire" culture   41
job change, aspects of   33–4
"light-touch" regulations of   40–2
logjam of talent, creation of   56–7
and mobility   37–9
national governments, efforts of   42–4
north to south trend   52–3
regulations for creation of   40–2
training scheme   43
for women   49–52
work culture and organization's values   31–2
"working for yourself" issues   148–9
working from home see home-working
working-age population, projected change in   5–7
workplaces
  best companies   104–7
  collective 'hive mind'   88–9
  connectivity rules   201–2
  eight cities, tale of   76–7
  and hubs for early adopters   95–6
  India without aircon   103–4
  in Middle East   72–5
  as model for the future   100–3
  offices, future of   93–5
  offices, place for   199–201
  overview of   75–6
  peer-to-peer   96–8
  of tomorrow   198–9
  virtual walls   85–8
  "what" you do, notion of   85
  work–life balance   85
World Vision   18

Xerox   68–9

Youth Development Fund   42
youth employment   38, 43, 62
Yunus, Muhammed   162; see also Group Lending/Grameen Model, concept of

Zurich   75, 77, 155, 158, 165, 187, 193

Printed and bound by CPI Group (UK) Ltd, Croydon, CR0 4YY